Getting Started with Red Hat Enterprise Virtualization

Leverage powerful Red Hat Enterprise Virtualization solutions to build your own IaaS cloud

Pradeep Subramanian

[PACKT] open source *
PUBLISHING   community experience distilled

BIRMINGHAM - MUMBAI

Getting Started with Red Hat Enterprise Virtualization

First published: September 2014

Production reference: 1190914

Published by Packt Publishing Ltd.
Livery Place
35 Livery Street
Birmingham B3 2PB, UK.

ISBN 978-1-78216-740-2

www.packtpub.com

Credits

Author
Pradeep Subramanian

Reviewers
Kyung Huh
René Koch
Anil Vettathu
Marcus Young

Commissioning Editor
Greg Wild

Acquisition Editor
Greg Wild

Content Development Editor
Athira Laji

Technical Editors
Shweta S. Pant
Humera Shaikh

Copy Editors
Mradula Hegde
Gladson Monteiro
Insiya Morbiwala
Aditya Nair
Adithi Shetty
Stuti Srivastava

Project Coordinator
Harshal Ved

Proofreader
Simran Bhogal

Indexer
Mariammal Chettiyar

Production Coordinator
Arvindkumar Gupta

Cover Work
Arvindkumar Gupta

About the Author

Pradeep Subramanian is a Senior Platform Consultant at Red Hat, a global provider of open source software solutions that uses a community-powered approach to develop and offer operating system, middleware, virtualization, storage, and cloud technologies. He has 10 years of experience in open source and Linux, which includes 5 years of extensive experience in open source virtualization technologies such as Xen, KVM, and Red Hat Enterprise Virtualization. His other areas of interest include high availability and grid computing, performance tuning, designing and building open hybrid cloud, architectural design, and implementation of Enterprise IT using open source tools. This is his first book.

I would like to express my gratitude to many people who saw me through this book. I would like to thank all those who provided their support, talked things over, read, wrote, offered comments, allowed me to quote their remarks, and assisted in the editing, proofreading, and designing of this book.

I owe a huge thanks to my manager, Anirudha Karandikar (Andy), for providing excellent support and advice. Above all, I want to thank my wife, Sandhya; my parents, Subramanian, Selvi, Shanmugam, Usha; and my naughty one-and-a-half-year-old son, Harsh. They all supported and encouraged me in spite of all the time the book took me away from them. It was a long and difficult journey for them. I am dedicating this book to my son, Harsh. I hope that one day, he will read this book and understand why I spent so much time in front of my computer. Last but not least, I beg forgiveness from all those who have been with me over the course of the years and whose names I have failed to mention. Thanks for everything; I look forward to writing the second edition of this book and a few more books on Open Cloud Computing soon!

About the Reviewers

Kyung Huh is currently working as a consultant in Korea. He has been working with Linux and open source software for more than 15 years as an instructor and consultant. He has experience in Red Hat Enterprise Virtualization in many production environments and also has experience in open source software such as clustering, performance tuning, and troubleshooting.

René Koch is a senior solution architect and consultant, focusing on open source virtualization, Linux, system management, and system monitoring. He started working with Red Hat Enterprise Virtualization and oVirt in 2010 and implemented various environments on the customer side. As part of the oVirt community, he is not only an active member on the oVirt mailing list, but also gives lectures about Red Hat Enterprise Virtualization and oVirt in Austria and Germany. Furthermore, he is the author of two open source projects: the Nagios plugin check_rhev3—which is used to monitor the whole RHEV environment with Nagios and Icinga—and Monitoring UI-Plugin—which is a user interface plugin for Red Hat Enterprise Virtualization and oVirt that integrates Nagios-based monitoring environments into the RHEV WebAdmin portal.

Anil Vettathu started his interaction with Linux in college. He started his career in 2006 as a Linux System Administrator. He has specialized in Open Source Virtualization technologies, especially KVM. He had the opportunity to work on RHEV from its very early versions. Currently, he is working as a TAM for Red Hat.

Marcus Young recently graduated with a degree in Computer Science and Mathematics before getting involved in system administration and DevOps. He currently works in software automation using open source tools and Red-Hat-flavored operating systems in RHEV and AWS virtualization environments. His hobbies include playing ice hockey and making homebrewed beer. He has also developed many hardware projects based on devices such as Arduino, Raspberry Pi, UDOO, and others.

I'd like to thank my beautiful fiancé for putting up with many of my projects and work items that make their way into my free time. I would also like to thank my newborn son who will continue to inspire me to keep pushing myself.

www.PacktPub.com

Support files, eBooks, discount offers, and more

You might want to visit www.PacktPub.com for support files and downloads related to your book.

Did you know that Packt offers eBook versions of every book published, with PDF and ePub files available? You can upgrade to the eBook version at www.PacktPub.com and as a print book customer, you are entitled to a discount on the eBook copy. Get in touch with us at service@packtpub.com for more details.

At www.PacktPub.com, you can also read a collection of free technical articles, sign up for a range of free newsletters and receive exclusive discounts and offers on Packt books and eBooks.

http://PacktLib.PacktPub.com

Do you need instant solutions to your IT questions? PacktLib is Packt's online digital book library. Here, you can access, read and search across Packt's entire library of books.

Why subscribe?

- Fully searchable across every book published by Packt
- Copy and paste, print and bookmark content
- On demand and accessible via web browser

Free access for Packt account holders

If you have an account with Packt at www.PacktPub.com, you can use this to access PacktLib today and view nine entirely free books. Simply use your login credentials for immediate access.

Table of Contents

Preface

Red Hat Enterprise Virtualization (RHEV), which is a complete enterprise virtualization management solution for servers and desktops, provides fully integrated management of your virtual infrastructures. RHEV is based on and built using two open source projects: Kernel Virtual Machine (KVM), which is open source software that comes with all standard Linux distributions, and oVirt. Based on the popular oVirt open virtualization management project, Red Hat Enterprise Virtualization positions itself as a strategic virtualization alternative to proprietary virtualization platforms with performance advantages, competitive pricing, and a trusted and stable environment.

Step-by-step, you'll learn how to build and manage Red Hat Enterprise Virtualization from scratch with various advanced features and troubleshooting steps. You'll also dive deep into the RHEV internal architecture and components.

What this book covers

Chapter 1, An Overview of Red Hat Enterprise Virtualization, gives you a basic introduction to RHEV, its internal architecture and components, and the basic hardware and software prerequisites.

Chapter 2, Installing RHEV Manager and Hypervisor Hosts, shows you how to set up and configure the RHEV Manager and access the web-based admin portal, install and configure RHEV's hypervisor hosts, and install and connect to the report portal in order to report scenarios of your virtual infrastructure's resource usage.

Chapter 3, Setting Up the RHEV Virtual Infrastructure, shows you how to create a virtual data center and cluster, add the hypervisor host to cluster, configure storage, and perform networking.

Chapter 4, Creating and Managing Virtual Machines, shows you how to create virtual machines, templates, derive virtual machines from the template, take live snapshots of virtual machines, and back up and restore of virtual machines using export and import disks.

Chapter 5, Virtual Machine and Host High Availability, shows you how to set up the virtual machine host availability, various cluster policies for cluster hosts, and perform live migration of virtual machines.

Chapter 6, Advanced Storage and Networking Features, briefs you about various storage disks options, such as sharing disks across virtual machines, direct LUN mapping from the storage, moving virtual machines across different storage domains, shaping the network traffic's VNIC profile for guest operating systems, and hot plugging of network adapter and memory into virtual machines.

Chapter 7, Quota and User Management, talks about applying quota to your virtualization infrastructure with user-role-based access control and integration with common directory services.

Chapter 8, Managing a Virtualization Environment from the Command Line, shows you how to set up the command-line tools in order to manage your virtualization infrastructure other than the standard RHEV Manager web-based interface.

Chapter 9, Troubleshooting RHEV, talks about various logfiles of the RHEV manager and hypervisor hosts and provides you with steps to put your RHEV virtualization infrastructure into maintenance mode for any planned outage.

Chapter 10, Setting Up iSCSI, NFS, and IdM Directory Services for RHEV, shows you how to set up your Red Hat Enterprise Linux server as an iSCSI, the NFS storage server for RHEV virtual machine data storage, the ISO library to store ISO, and export the domain to export the virtual machine for backup and restoration, and set up and configure IdM directory services on RHEL to integrate RHEV with the Red Hat IdM directory service for user management.

Appendix shows you how to upgrade RHEV environment from Version 3.3 to 3.4. This chapter is available as a bonus chapter and can be downloaded from `https://www.packtpub.com/sites/default/files/downloads/7402OS_Appendix.pdf`.

What you need for this book

To set up a demo environment for this book, you need a valid Red Hat account to access the Red Hat software and support portal or, optionally, an evaluation version of RHEV:

- `https://access.redhat.com/downloads/`
- `https://access.redhat.com/products/red-hat-enterprise-virtualization#evaluations`

Please note that the current RHEV GA release is 3.4, but the book is based on a 3.3 release. So if you access the preceding evaluation link, it will direct you to 3.4. Please create an evaluation account, log in to `https://access.redhat.com/downloads/`, and choose the RHEV Manager channel rhel-x86_64-server-6-rhevm-3.3 for the manager deployment.

You will also need the following set of hardware and software in order to run the examples in this book.

Red Hat Enterprise Virtualization Manager 3.3

The following are the hardware and software requirements of the Red Hat Enterprise Virtualization manager 3.3:

- **Hardware**: The commodity's physical hardware or virtual machine
- **Operating system**: Red Hat Enterprise Linux 6 Update 5
- **Software channels**:
  - rhel-x86_64-server-6-rhevm-3.3
  - rhel-x86_64-server-supplementary-6 -c
  - jbappplatform-6-x86_64-server-6-rpm

The Red Hat Enterprise Virtualization Hypervisor host

The following are the hardware and software requirements of the Red Hat Enterprise Virtualization Hypervisor host:

- **Hardware**: Commodity virtualization-enabled physical hardware supports Red Hat Enterprise Linux 6 Update 5
- **Software**: RHEV-H image (for RHEV-M 3.3) — downloadable from `https://access.redhat.com/downloads/`

Optional requirements

The following are the optional requirements that are needed to run the examples in this book:

- Red Hat IdM Directory Service:
    - **Hardware**: The commodity physical hardware or virtual machine that acts as a directory server
    - **Operating System**: Red Hat Enterprise Linux 6 Update 5
    - **Software**: Identity management (ships by default)

- ISCSI / NFS storage service:
    - **Hardware**: The commodity physical hardware or virtual machine that acts as a storage
    - **Operating system**: Red Hat Enterprise Linux 6 Update 5
    - **Software**: NFS/iSCSI-related package ships with default operating systems

Who this book is for

If you are a system administrator who is interested in implementing and managing open source virtualization infrastructures, this is the book for you. You need a basic knowledge of virtualization and its use cases and some very basic Linux command-line work experience.

Conventions

In this book, you will find a number of styles of text that distinguish between different kinds of information. Here are some examples of these styles, and an explanation of their meaning.

Code words in text, database table names, folder names, filenames, file extensions, pathnames, dummy URLs, user input, and Twitter handles are shown as follows: "This command will switch off SELinux enforcement temporarily until the machine is rebooted. If you would like to permanently disable it, edit `/etc/sysconfig/selinux` and enter `SELINUX=disabled`."

Any command-line input or output is written as follows:

```
# rhn-channel -a -c rhel-x86_64-server-6-rhevm-3.3 -c rhel-x86_64-server-
supplementary-6 -c jbappplatform-6-x86_64-server-6-rpm
Username: "yourrhnlogin"
Password: XXXX
```

New terms and **important words** are shown in bold. Words that you see on the screen, in menus or dialog boxes for example, appear in the text like this: "Finally, label the ISO domain with a name that will be unique and easily identifiable on the **Storage** tab of the administration portal".

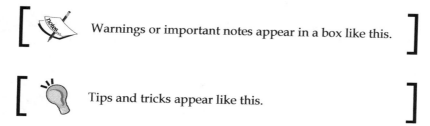

Warnings or important notes appear in a box like this.

Tips and tricks appear like this.

Reader feedback

Feedback from our readers is always welcome. Let us know what you think about this book—what you liked or may have disliked. Reader feedback is important for us to develop titles that you really get the most out of.

To send us general feedback, simply send an e-mail to feedback@packtpub.com, and mention the book title via the subject of your message.

If there is a topic that you have expertise in and you are interested in either writing or contributing to a book, see our author guide on www.packtpub.com/authors.

Customer support

Now that you are the proud owner of a Packt book, we have a number of things to help you to get the most from your purchase.

Downloading the example code

You can download the example code files for all Packt books you have purchased from your account at http://www.packtpub.com. If you purchased this book elsewhere, you can visit http://www.packtpub.com/support and register to have the files e-mailed directly to you.

Errata

Although we have taken every care to ensure the accuracy of our content, mistakes do happen. If you find a mistake in one of our books—maybe a mistake in the text or the code—we would be grateful if you would report this to us. By doing so, you can save other readers from frustration and help us improve subsequent versions of this book. If you find any errata, please report them by visiting http://www.packtpub.com/submit-errata, selecting your book, clicking on the **errata submission form** link, and entering the details of your errata. Once your errata are verified, your submission will be accepted and the errata will be uploaded on our website, or added to any list of existing errata, under the Errata section of that title. Any existing errata can be viewed by selecting your title from http://www.packtpub.com/support.

Piracy

Piracy of copyright material on the Internet is an ongoing problem across all media. At Packt, we take the protection of our copyright and licenses very seriously. If you come across any illegal copies of our works, in any form, on the Internet, please provide us with the location address or website name immediately so that we can pursue a remedy.

Please contact us at copyright@packtpub.com with a link to the suspected pirated material.

We appreciate your help in protecting our authors, and our ability to bring you valuable content.

Questions

You can contact us at questions@packtpub.com if you are having a problem with any aspect of the book, and we will do our best to address it.

1
An Overview of Red Hat Enterprise Virtualization

This introductory chapter will help you understand the following things before deploying and managing **Red Hat Enterprise Virtualization (RHEV)**:

- Virtualization and its basic concepts
- An overview of Kernel-based Virtual Machine (KVM) RHEV
- The RHEV architecture and its components
- Hardware and software prerequisites

The virtualization overview

Hardware virtualization or platform virtualization allows multiple operating system instances to run concurrently on a single computer. This is a means of separating hardware from a single operating system. A hypervisor or **Virtual Machine Monitor (VMM)** is a piece of computer software that runs on host machine, which will allow you to create and manage the virtual machine on top of the host. The hypervisor virtualizes all resources (for example, processors, memory, storage, and networks) and allocates them to the various virtual machines that run on top of the hypervisor. In general, physical hardware that runs the hypervisor software is called the host machine and the virtual machine is called the guest operating system.

Consider an example of a computer that is running a production application server on Red Hat Enterprise Linux. The developer needs to test and implement new features. In a typical scenario without any virtualization, there will be dedicated physical hardware for the production and development environment. Virtualization allows you to run both production and development instances of your application in complete isolation from one another on the same physical hardware. As the virtualization hypervisor software sits between the guest and the hardware, it can control the guests' use of CPU, memory, storage, and network between these two environments.

Kernel-based Virtual Machine (KVM)

Kernel-based Virtual Machine is an open source hypervisor solution (`http://www.linux-kvm.org/page/Main_Page`) for Linux that supports x86, PowerPC, and S390 CPU architecture that contains virtualization extensions. KVM uses the hardware virtualization support of these processors and effectively turns your Linux kernel into a bare metal hypervisor. It supports a mixed workload of various guest operating systems that run your applications on Linux and Windows in order to host critical and noncritical applications. Many current Linux distributions ship KVM and the Red-Hat-included KVM hypervisor technology in a release of Red Hat Enterprise Linux Version 5 update 4 and its later release.

KVM outperforms other virtualization hypervisors in various virtualization scenarios, and it has top scores in the SPECvirt_2010 virtualization benchmark. It includes the overall top performance scores and the highest number of performant VMs running on a single hypervisor. KVM is free software that was released under the GPL, and it's a powerful open source hypervisor solution alternative to the VMware, Citrix Xen, and Hyper-V RHEV overview.

The RHEV platform is an enterprise-grade, centralized-management hypervisor for server and desktop virtualization. It's a complete virtualization management solution that provides fully integrated management of your virtual infrastructures. The RHEV platform includes two major components: Red Hat Enterprise Virtualization Manager, which is a centralized management server, and optimized KVM hypervisor software, which hosts the virtual machines.

Red Hat supports RHEV through the subscription model, which provides enterprise-ready solutions that can be confidently deployed to manage even your most mission-critical applications. Red Hat subscription gives you access to the Red Hat customer portal (`https://access.redhat.com`) and provides simple, integrated access to all features of your subscription. Users can open support tickets, read and download the documentation, and find useful information in the knowledge base.

RHEV is based on the KVM hypervisor and the upstream **oVirt** open virtualization management platform, which is a project started by Red Hat and released to the open source community (http://www.ovirt.org/Home). oVirt is the community-supported open source project. It will be the baseline of RHEV products, and it's very similar to RHEL, which is based on the Fedora distro.

Features of RHEV

With RHEV, you can virtualize even the most demanding application workloads with features including the following:

- **Host scalability**: This supports a limit of up to 160 logical CPUs and 2 TB per host (platform capable of up to 4,096 logical CPUs / 64 TB per host)
- **Guest scalability**: This supports up to 160 vCPU and 2 TB VRAM per guest
- **KSM memory over commitment**: This allows administrators to define more RAM in their VMs than what is present in a physical host
- **Security**: This supports SELinux and new sVirt capabilities, including **Mandatory Access Control (MAC)** for enhanced virtual machine and hypervisor security
- **Management**: This provides centralized enterprise-grade virtualization management engines with a graphical administration console and programming interfaces
- **Live migration**: This allows running virtual machines to be moved seamlessly from one host to another
- **High availability**: This allows critical VMs to be restarted on another host in the event of hardware failure with three levels of priority
- **System scheduler**: This provides system scheduler policies for load balancing to automatically balance the VM load among hosts in a cluster
- **Power saver**: The power saver mode is used to consolidate VM loads onto fewer hosts during nonpeak hours
- **Maintenance manager**: This allows you to move the hypervisor into the maintenance mode for any software or hardware updates of the hypervisor
- **Image management**: This supports template-based provisioning, live virtual machine snapshots, and cloning new virtual machines from snapshots
- **Monitoring and reporting**: This provides a suite of preconfigured reports and dashboards and creates your own ad hoc reports that enable you to monitor the system

- **OVF import/export**: This allows you to import and export **Open Virtualization Format (OVF)** virtual machines into RHEV
- **V2V**: This automates the conversion of the VMware or Xen virtual machine images into an OVF file for use within RHEV

Supported virtual machine operating systems

RHEV supports a wide range of Linux and Windows operating systems that can be virtualized as guest operating systems.

 Refer to http://www.redhat.com/resourcelibrary/ articles/enterprise-linux-virtualization-support for information on the up-to-date guest support.

RHEV architecture

The RHEV platform comprises multiple components that work seamlessly together, as represented in the following diagram, and each component is explained in detail under the *Components of RHEV* section:

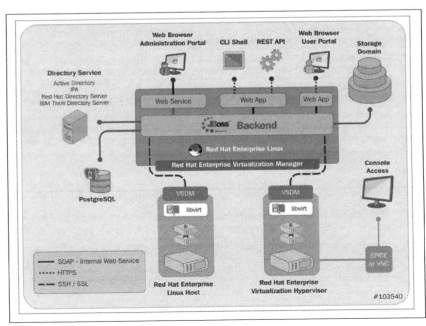

Components of RHEV

The RHEV platform consists of the following components:

- **Red Hat Enterprise Virtualization Manager (RHEV-M)**: This is a centralized management console with a graphical, web-based interface that manages your complete virtualization infrastructure, such as hosts, storage, network, virtual machines, and more, running on the physical hardware.

- **Red Hat Enterprise Virtualization Hypervisor (RHEV-H)**: RHEV hosts can be either based on full Red Hat Enterprise Linux 6 systems with KVM enabled (also called Red Hat Enterprise Linux Virtualization Hosts) or on purpose-built RHEV-H hosts. RHEV-H is a bare metal, image-based, small-footprint (less than 200 MB) hypervisor with minimized security footprint, also referred to as Red Hat Enterprise Virtualization Hypervisor.

  What is the difference between these two? RHEV-H is like a live image that does not allow third-party applications, whereas the RHEL host is an operating system with KVM modules that allows any third-party software.

- **Virtual Desktop and Server Management Daemon (VDSM)**: This runs as the VDSM service on the RHEV hypervisor host that facilitates the communication between RHEV-M and the hypervisor host. It uses the libvirt (http://libvirt.org/) and QEMU service for the management and monitoring of virtual machines and other resources such as hosts, networking, storage, and so on.

- **Storage domains**: This is used to store virtual machine images, snapshots, templates, and ISO disk images in order to spin up virtual machines.

- **Logical networking**: This defines virtual networking for guest data, storage access, and management and displays network that accesses the virtual machine consoles.

- **Database platform**: This is used to store information about the state of virtualization environment.

- **SPICE**: This is an open remote computing protocol that provides client access to remote virtual machine display and devices (keyboard, mouse, and audio). VNC can also be used to get remote console access.

- **Authentication**: This provides integration with external directory services such as Red Hat IPA and Active Directory Services for user authentication.

- **API support**: RHEV v3.3 and higher supports the REST API, Python SDK, and Java Software Development Kit, which allow users to perform complete automation of managing virtualization infrastructure outside of a standard web interface of manager using own programs or custom scripts. Users can also use command-line shell utility to interact with RHEV-M outside of the standard web interface in order to manage your virtual infrastructure.

- **Admin/user portal**: This is used for initial setup, configuration, and management. There is a power user portal, which is a trimmed-down version of the administration portal that is tailored for the end user's self-provisioning of virtual machines.

The hardware and software requirement of RHEV

The following section explains the minimal hardware and software requirements in order to install, set up, and run RHEV in your environment.

Red Hat Enterprise Virtualization Manager

In order to deploy and set up RHEV-M on a physical or virtual machine, the following are the minimum or recommended hardware prerequisites:

Minimum requirements:

- A dual-core CPU
- 4 GB of RAM
- 25 GB local disk space
- Network Interface Card with bandwidth of 1 GBps

Recommended requirements:

- A quad-core CPU
- 16 GB of RAM
- 50 GB local disk space
- Network Interface Card with bandwidth of 1 GBps

RHEV-M requires the Red Hat Enterprise Linux 6.3 server or higher. Install only minimal or basic server type during the installation in order to avoid package conflict while setting up the manager.

A valid Red Hat Network subscription uses RHN classic to access the following channels. It is highly recommended that you the Red Hat subscription manager to subscribe to these relevant channels. However, the following channel names will vary if you use the subscription manager. In this book, we use RHN classic to register and subscribe to the following channels later during our manager setup:

- Red Hat Enterprise Linux Server (v6 for 64-bit x86_64)
- RHEL Server Supplementary (v6 64-bit x86_64)
- Red Hat Enterprise Virtualization Manager (v3.3 x86_64)
- Red Hat JBoss EAP (v6) for 6Server x86_64

The Red Hat Enterprise Virtualization Hypervisor host

One or two physical hosts act as virtualization hosts or RHEV-H. A minimum of two hypervisor hosts is required to demonstrate and test the live migration of virtual machines across hypervisor hosts.

Intel or AMD 64-bit supported hardware with virtualization extensions support of Intel VT or AMD-V enabled with following minimal compute requirements:

- 2 GB RAM
- 2 GB local disk space
- One network interface with a bandwidth of 1 GBps

The recommended hardware for virtualization hosts always varies as per your requirement. Consider the following basic factors before sizing your hardware:

- The number of guest operating systems, their application memory, and CPU requirements. For network-intensive application workloads, add multiple network interfaces and segregate the network traffic using RHEV's logical networks.
- For less critical and non-disk I/O-intensive applications, use local storage, and in this case, extend the internal storage size of virtualization hosts in order to store the virtual machine images as per your requirement. However, keep in mind that the use of local storage will prevent other features such as live migration of virtual machines to other hosts.
- For high transnational database workloads, use the NAS/SAN storage with a dedicated network interface in the case of NAS and FC for SAN.
- Virtualization hosts must run Version 6.3 or higher of either the RHEV hypervisor host or Red Hat Enterprise Linux Server as a host.

The Red Hat Enterprise Virtualization Manager client

In order to access the manager, you need the following supported clients and browsers:

- Mozilla Firefox 17 or higher is required to access both portals on Red Hat Enterprise Linux.

- Internet Explorer 8 or higher is required to access the user portal on Microsoft Windows. Use the desktop version and not the touchscreen version of Internet Explorer 10.

- Internet Explorer 9 or higher is required to access the administration portal on Microsoft Windows. Use the desktop version and not the touchscreen version of Internet Explorer 10. It's possible to access the manager portal from other browsers, but it's not tested and supported. Similarly, tablet and touchscreen versions of browsers are also not supported and tested at the time of writing this book.

Install a supported SPICE client in order to access virtual machine consoles. Check the Red Hat Enterprise Virtualization Manager release notes to see which SPICE features your client supports.

Storage

You need a storage type of NFS, ISCSI, SAN, POSIX, Red Hat Storage (GlusterFS), or local storage for data domains to store virtual machine images. The NFS system is required in order to store your ISO library and to export and import virtual machines for complete image backup and restoration of virtual machine images.

Directory services (optional)

While setting up RHEV-M, the RHEV-M installer script will create its own internal admin user for the initial configuration and setup. To add more users, you need to attach the manager to one of the supported directory services:

- Active Directory Red Hat **Identity Management** (**IdM**)
- Red Hat Directory Server 9 (RHDS 9)
- OpenLDAP

Networking and Domain Name Service

For the host networking and fully qualified domain name resolution, you need the following:

- A static IP address for RHEV-M and for each hypervisor host management network.

- A DNS service that can resolve both forward and DNS entries for those static IP addresses.

- An optional existing DHCP server that can address the network address for the virtual machine.

Virtual machines

We need installation images in order to create virtual machines and their valid license or subscription entitlement for each operating system. We will use these ISO images and later upload them to the ISO domain in order to use them as an installation media that deploys the operating system on a virtual machine.

Firewall Requirements

The RHEV infrastructure requires that the network traffic on a number of ports be allowed through the firewall. The following is the list of required ports that are to be opened on the firewall across various RHEV components.

Virtualization manager firewall requirements

RHEV-M requires the following ports be opened in order to allow network traffic through the system's firewall:

Source	Destination	Port/Protocol	Purpose
The hypervisor host	RHEV-M	ICMP	RHEV-M verifies the hypervisor's reachability via ICMP after the initial host registration
The remote client	RHEV-M	22/TCP	To provide SSH access to the manager
Admin / User portal clients / Hypervisor host	RHEV-M	80 and 443/TCP	To access the admin and user portal from remote clients

If you plan to use the NFS ISO storage domain on the same box as the running RHEV-M in order to store your ISO library to create virtual machines, please open TCP port 2049 for NFSv4.

Virtualization host firewall requirements

The Red Hat Enterprise Virtualization Hosts require the following ports be opened in order to allow the network traffic through the system's firewall:

Source	Destination	Port/Protocol	Purpose
RHEV-M	Hypervisor Hosts	22	To secure shell access
Admin / User portal clients	Hypervisor Hosts	From 5900 to 6411/ TCP	Used for Spice/VNC console access
Hypervisor Hosts	Hypervisor Hosts	16514/TCP	Used for libvirt virtual machine migration
Hypervisor Hosts	Hypervisor Hosts	From 49152 to 49216/TCP	Used for virtual machine migration and fencing
Hypervisor Hosts / RHEV-M	Hypervisor Hosts	54321/TCP	To provide VDSM communication with manager and hypervisors

Directory server firewall requirements

The following ports are to be opened if you wish to integrate RHEV-M with directory services for user authentication:

Source	Destination	Port/Protocol	Purpose
RHEV-M	Directory server	88 and 463/(TCP/UDP)	Used for the Kerberos authentication
RHEV-M	Directory server	389 and 636/TCP	**Lightweight Directory Access Protocol (LDAP)** and LDAPS over SSL

Remote database server firewall requirements

The following ports are to be opened if you wish to use the remote PostgreSQL database instance with RHEV-M:

Source	Destination	Port/Protocol	Purpose
RHEV-M	Remote PostgreSQL database server	5432/(TCP and UDP)	Used as a default port for PostgreSQL database connections

User accounts and groups

The following users and groups are created by the RHEV-M setup tool in order to support virtualization on the manager system. If existing UIDs and GIDs on the host conflict with the default values used during the VDSM and QEMU installation, a conflict occurs.

Users	Group
• VDSM (UID: 36)	• KVM (GID: 36)
• oVirt (UID: 108)	• oVirt (GID: 108)

The following users and groups are created by default on the hypervisor when installing VDSM and QEMU packages. If existing UIDs and GIDs on the host conflict with the default values used during the installation, a conflict occurs.

Users	Group
• VDSM (UID: 36)	• KVM (GID: 36)
• QEUM (UID: 107)	• QEUM (GID: 107)
• Sanlock (UID: 179)	

RHEV 3.3 supports a self-hosted engine of RHEV-M, which enables RHEV-M to be run as a virtual machine on the hypervisor hosts it manages in an HA configuration. This will reduce the dependency on the dedicated physical or virtual hardware that hosts your RHEV-M instance.

For more information, refer to Red Hat Enterprise Virtualization Manager 3.3 Release notes at https://access.redhat.com/documentation/en-US/Red_Hat_Enterprise_Virtualization/3.3/html-single/Manager_Release_Notes/index.html.

Summary

In this chapter, we discussed the basic concept of virtualization and were introduced to the Linux kernel virtual machine. We then moved further with an introduction to Red Hat Enterprise Virtualization and its relation to KVM. Then, we learned about the detailed architecture, components, and hardware and software requirements of Red Hat Enterprise Virtualization for better planning in order to design your first Red Hat Enterprise Virtualization infrastructure.

In the next chapter, we will learn how to install and configure RHEV Manager and hypervisor hosts. This will also explain how to manage your virtual infrastructure from the admin web interface and access the reporting from the report portal.

2

Installing RHEV Manager and Hypervisor Hosts

This chapter describes setting up RHEV-M, including the installation, initial configuration, and connection to the administrator and user portal of the manager web interface.

In the latter part of the chapter, we will learn how to deploy and configure the hypervisor and set up the RHEV-M report portal.

Here are some of the major areas we are going to cover in the rest of this chapter:

- Setting up the Red Hat Enterprise Linux operating system for the manager
- Installing and configuring RHEV-M and reporting
- Connecting to the administration (admin) and user portal
- Deploying the RHEV-H host on the physical server

Environment mapping

The following table lists **Fully Qualified Domain Names (FQDN)**, associated IP details, and the server roles used in the rest of the chapters to set up the Red Hat Enterprise Virtualization infrastructure:

FQDN	IP	Role
rhevmanager.example.com	192.168.100.80	RHEV-M
hypervisor1.example.com	192.168.100.81	RHEV-H host 1
hypervisor2.example.com	192.168.100.82	RHEV-H host 2
iscsi-storage.example.com	192.168.100.83	RHEL iSCSI storage server
ipa.example.com	192.168.100.84	RHEL Identity Management

Setting up the RHEL operating system for the manager

Prior to starting the installation of RHEV-M, please make sure all the prerequisites are met as explained in *Chapter 1, An Overview of Red Hat Enterprise Virtualization.*

Consider the following when setting up RHEL OS for RHEV-M:

- Install Red Hat Enterprise Linux 6 with latest minor update of 5, and during package selection step, select minimal or basic server as an option. Don't select any custom package.
- The hostname should be set to FQDN.
- Set up basic networking; use of static IP is recommended for your manager with a default gateway and primary and secondary DNS client configured.
- SELinux and iptables are enabled by default as part of the operating system installation. For more security, it's highly recommended to keep it on.

To disable SELinux on Red Hat Enterprise Linux, please run the following command as the root user:

```
# setenforce Permissive
```

This command will switch off SELinux enforcement temporarily until the machine is rebooted. If you would like to permanently disable it, edit `/etc/sysconfig/selinux` and enter `SELINUX=disabled`.

Registering with Red Hat Network

To install RHEV-M, you need to first register your manager machine with Red Hat Network and subscribe to the relevant channels.

> You need to connect your machine to the Red Hat Network with a valid account with access to the relevant software channels to register your machine and deploy RHEV-M packages.

If your environment does not have access to the Red Hat Network, you can perform an offline installation of RHEV-M. For more information, please refer to `https://access.redhat.com/site/articles/216983`.

To register your machine with the Red Hat Network using RHN Classic, please run the following command from the shell and follow the onscreen instructions:

```
# rhn_register
```

This command will register your manager machine to the parent channel of your operating system version. It's strongly recommended to use Red Hat Subscription Manager to register and subscribe to the relevant channel. To use Red Hat Subscription Manager, please refer to the *Subscribing to the Red Hat Enterprise Virtualization Manager Channels using Subscription Manager* section from the RHEV 3.3 installation guide at `https://access.redhat.com/documentation/en-US/Red_Hat_Enterprise_Virtualization/3.3/html/Installation_Guide/index.html`.

After successful registration of your manager machine to the Red Hat Network, subscribe the manager machine using the following command to subscribe to the relevant channels. Then download and install the manager-related software packages. The following command will prompt you to enter your Red Hat Network login credentials:

```
# rhn-channel -a -c rhel-x86_64-server-6-rhevm-3.3 -c rhel-x86_64-server-
supplementary-6 -c jbappplatform-6-x86_64-server-6-rpm
Username: "yourrhnlogin"
Password: XXXX
```

To cross-check whether your manager machine is registered with Red Hat Network and subscribed to the relevant channels, please run the following command. This will return all the channels mentioned earlier plus the base channel of your operating system version, as shown in the following yum command output:

```
# yum repolist
repo id                                              repo name
status

jbappplatform-6-x86_64-server-6-rpm                  Red Hat JBoss EAP (v
6) for 6Server x86_64                                    1,415

rhel-x86_64-server-6                                 Red Hat Enterprise
Linux Server (v. 6 for 64-bit x86_64)                   12,662

rhel-x86_64-server-6-rhevm-3.3                       Red Hat Enterprise
Virtualization Manager (v.3.3 x86_64)                   164

rhel-x86_64-server-supplementary-6                   RHEL Server
Supplementary (v. 6 64-bit x86_64)                      370
```

You are now ready to start downloading and installing the software required to set up and run your RHEV-M.

Installing the RHEV-Manager packages

Update your Red Hat Enterprise Linux operating system to the latest up-to-date version by running the following command:

```
# yum -y upgrade
```

Reboot the machine if the upgrade installed the latest version of the kernel.

After a successful upgrade, run the following command to install RHEV-M and its dependent packages:

```
# yum -y install rhevm
```

There are a few conditions you need to consider before configuring RHEV-M:

- We need a working DNS for forward and reverse lookup of FQDN. We are going to use the Red Hat IdM server configured with the DNS role in the rest of the chapter for domain name resolution of the entire virtualization infrastructure. Please refer to *Chapter 10, Setting Up iSCSI, NFS, and IdM Directory Services for RHEV*, to set up the basic IdM server on RHEL 6. Refer to the Red Hat **Identity Management Guide** for more information on how to add forward and reverse zone records to the configured IdM DNS at https://access.redhat.com/documentation/en-US/Red_Hat_Enterprise_Linux/6/html/Identity_Management_Guide/Working_with_DNS.html.

 You can't install Identity Management software on the same box where the manager is going to be deployed due to some package conflicts.

- To store ISO images of operating systems in order to create a virtual machine, you need **Network File Server (NFS)** with a planned NFS export path. If your manager machine has sufficient storage space to host all your ISOs, you can set up the ISO domain while configuring the manager to set up the NFS share automatically through the installer to store all your ISO images. If you have an existing NFS server, it's recommended to use a dedicated export for the ISO domain to store the ISO images instead of using the manager server to serve the NFS service.

- Here we are going to use a dedicated local mount point named /rhev-iso-library on the RHEV Manager box to store our ISO images to provision the virtual machine. Note that the mount point should be empty and only contain the user and group ownership and permission sets before running the installer:

```
# chown -R 36:36 /rhev-iso-library ;  chmod 0755 /rhev-iso-library
```

It will also be useful to have the following information at hand:

- Ports to be used for HTTP and HTTPS communication.
- FQDN of the manager. A reverse lookup is performed on your hostname.
- At the time of writing this book, RHEV supported only the PostgreSQL database for use with RHEV-M. You can use a local database or remote database setup. Here we are going to use the local database. In the case of a remote database setup, keep all database login credentials ready.

 Please refer to the *Preparing a PostgreSQL Database for Use with Red Hat Enterprise Virtualization Manager* section for detailed information on setting up a remote database to use with manager at `https://access.redhat.com/documentation/en-US/Red_Hat_Enterprise_Virtualization/3.3/html-single/Installation_Guide/index.html#Preparing_a_Postgres_Database_Server_for_use_with_Red_Hat_Enterprise_Virtualization_Manager`.

- Password for internal admin account of RHEV-M.
- Organization name for the RHEV-M SSL certificate.
- Leave the default storage type to NFS for the initial default data center. We will create a new data center in the latter stage of our setup.
- Provide the file system path and display name for NFS ISO library configuration, so that the manager will configure NFS of the supplied filesystem path, and make it visible by the display name under the **Storage** tab section on administration portal of RHEV-M.

Running the initial engine setup

Once you're prepared with all the answers to the questions we discussed in the previous section, it's time to run the initial configuration script called `engine-setup` to perform the initial configuration and setting up of RHEV-M. The installer will ask you several questions, which have been discussed above and based on your input, it will configure your RHEV-M. Leave the default settings as they are and press *Enter* if you feel the installer's default answers are appropriate to your setup. Once the installer takes in all your input, it will ask you for the final confirmation of your supplied configuration setting; type in `OK` and press *Enter* to continue the setup. For better understanding, please refer to the following output of the `engine-setup` installer while setting up a lab for this chapter.

Log in to manager as the root user, and from the shell of your Manager machine, run the following `engine-setup` command:

```
# engine-setup
```

Once you execute this command, engine-setup performs the following set of tasks on the system:

- First check whether any updates are available for this system. Accept the default `Yes` and proceed further:

  ```
  Checking for product updates and update if available. Enter
  Default Yes.
  ```

- Set the hostname of the RHEV-M system. The administration portal web access will get bound to the FQDN entered here:

  ```
  Host fully qualified DNS name of this server [rhevmanager.example.
  com]:
  ```

- Set up the firewall rule on the manager system, and this will backup your existing firewall rule configured on the manager system if any:

  ```
  Do you want Setup to configure the firewall? (Yes, No) [Yes]: No
  ```

- `Local` will set up the PostgreSQL database instance on the manager system; optionally, you can choose `Remote` to use the existing remote PostgreSQL database instance to use with manager:

  ```
  Where is the database located? (Local, Remote) [Local]:
  ```

- If you selected `Local`, you will get an option to customize the PostgreSQL database setup by choosing the relevant option:

  ```
  Would you like Setup to automatically configure PostgreSQL, or
  prefer to perform that manually? (Automatic, Manual) [Automatic]:
  ```

- Set up the internal admin user password to access the manager web interface for initial setup of the virtualization infrastructure:

  ```
  Engine admin password:
  ```
  ```
  Confirm engine admin password:
  ```

- RHEV supports the use of clusters to manage Gluster storage bricks in addition to virtualization hosts. Choosing both will give the flexibility to use hypervisor hosts to host virtual machines as well as other sets of hypervisor hosts to manage Gluster storage bricks in your RHEV environment:

  ```
  Application mode (Both, Virt, Gluster) [Both]:
  ```

- Engine installer creates a data center named `Default` as part of the initial setup. The following step will ask you to select the type of storage to be used with the data center. Mixing storage domains of different types is not supported in the 3.3 release, but it is supported in the latest 3.4 release. Choose the default `NFS` option and proceed further. We are going to create a new data center, using the administration portal, from scratch after the engine setup and then select the storage type as `ISCSI` for the rest of this book:

  ```
  Default storage type: (NFS, FC, ISCSI, POSIXFS) [NFS]:
  ```

- The manager uses certificates to communicate securely with its hosts. Provide your organization's name for the certificate:

  ```
  Organization name for certificate [example.com]:
  ```

- The manager uses the Apache web server to present a landing page to users. The `engine-setup` script can make the landing page of the manager the default page presented by Apache:

  ```
  Do you wish to set the application as the default page of the web
  server? (Yes, No) [Yes]:
  ```

- By default, external SSL (HTTPS) communications with the manager are secured with the self-signed certificate created in the PKI configuration stage for secure communication with hosts. Another certificate may be chosen for external HTTPS connections without affecting how the manager communicates with hosts:

  ```
  Setup can configure apache to use SSL using a certificate issued
  from the internal CA.

  Do you wish Setup to configure that, or prefer to perform that
  manually? (Automatic, Manual) [Automatic]:
  ```

- Choose `Yes` to set up an NFS share on the manager system and provide the export path to be used to dump the ISO images in a later part. Finally, label the ISO domain with a name that will be unique and easily identifiable on the **Storage** tab of the administration portal:

  ```
  Configure an NFS share on this server to be used as an ISO Domain?
  (Yes, No) [Yes]:

  Local ISO domain path [/var/lib/exports/iso]: /rhev-iso-library

  Local ISO domain name [ISO_DOMAIN]: ISO_Datastore
  ```

- The `engine-setup` script can optionally configure a WebSocket proxy server in order to allow users to connect with virtual machines via the noVNC or HTML 5 consoles:

  ```
  Configure WebSocket Proxy on this machine? (Yes, No) [Yes]:
  ```

- The final step will ask you to provide proxy server credentials if the manager system is hosted behind the proxy server to access the Internet. RHEV supports vRed Hat Access Plugin, which will help you collect the logs and open a service request with Red Hat Global Support Services from the administration portal of the manager:

  ```
  Would you like transactions from the Red Hat Access Plugin sent
  from the RHEV Manager to be brokered through a proxy server? (Yes,
  No) [No]:
  ```

- Finally, if you feel all the input and configurations are satisfactory, press *Enter* to complete the engine setup.

- It will show you the configuration preview, and if you feel satisfied, press OK:

  ```
  Please confirm installation settings (OK, Cancel) [OK]:
  ```

After the successful setup of RHEV-M, you can see the summary, which will show various bits of information such as how to access the admin portal of RHEV-M, the installed logs, the configured iptables firewall, the required ports, and so on.

Connecting to the admin and user portal 006C

Now access the admin portal, as shown in the following screenshot, using the following URLs:

- `http://rhevmanager.example.com:80/ovirt-engine`
- `https://rhevmanager.example.com:443/ovirt-engine`

Use the user admin and password specified during the setup to log in to the oVirt engine (also called RHEV-M).

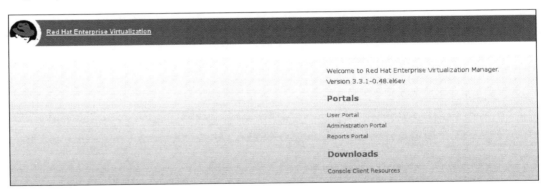

1. Click on **Administration Portal** and log in using the credentials you set up for the admin account during the engine setup.

2. Then click on **User Portal** and log in using the credentials you set up for the admin account during the engine setup. You will see a difference in the portal with a very trimmed-down user interface that is useful for self-service.

We will see how to integrate the manager with other active directory services and efficiently use the user portal for self-service consumption later in the book.

RHEV reporting

RHEV bundles two optional components. The first is the history management database, which holds the historical information of various virtualization resources such as data centers, clusters, hosts, virtual machines, and others so that any other external application can consume them for reporting.

The second optional component is the customized JasperServer and JasperReports. JasperServer is an open source reporting tool capable of generating and exporting reports in various formats such as PDF, Word, and CSV for end user consumption.

To enable the reporting functionality, you need to install the specific components that we discussed. For simplicity, we are installing both the components at one go using the command described in the following section.

Installing the RHEV history database and report server

To install the history database and report servers, execute the following command:

```
# yum install rhevm-dwh   rhevm-reports
```

Once you have installed the reporting components, you need to start with setting up the RHEV history database by using the following command:

```
# rhevm-dwh-setup
```

This will momentarily stop and start the oVirt engine service during the setup. Further, it will ask you to create a read-only user account to access the history database. Create it if you want to allow remote access to the history database and follow the onscreen instructions and finish the setup.

Once the oVirt engine history database (also known as the RHEV Manager history database) is created, move on to setting up the report server. From the RHEV-M server, run the following command to set up the reporting server:

```
# rhevm-reports-setup
#setup will prompt to restart ovirt-engine service.
In order to proceed the installer must stop the ovirt-engine service
Would you like to stop the ovirt-engine service? (yes|no):
#The command then performs a number of actions before prompting you
to set the password for the Red Hat Enterprise Virtualization Manager
Reports administrative users (rhevm-admin and superuser)
Please choose a password for the reports admin user(s) (rhevm-admin and
superuser):
```

Downloading the example code

You can download the example code files for all Packt books you have purchased from your account at http://www.packtpub.com. If you purchased this book elsewhere, you can visit http://www.packtpub.com/support and register to have the files e-mailed directly to you.

Follow the onscreen instructions and enter `Yes` to stop the oVirt-engine and set up a password for the default internal super user account called `rhevm-admin` to access and manage the report portal and proceed further with the setup. Note that this user is different from the internal admin account we set up during the engine setup of RHEV-M. The `rhevm-admin` user is used only for accessing and managing the report portal, not for the admin or user portal.

Accessing the RHEV report portal

After the successful installation and initial configuration setup of the report portal, you can access it by https://rhevmanager.example.com/rhevm-reports/login.html from your client machine. You can also access the report portal from the manager web interface by clicking on the **Reports Portal** hyperlink, which will redirect you to the report portal.

Log in with `rhevm-admin` and the password credentials we set while running the RHEV-M report setup script in the previous section to generate reports and create and manage users to access the report portal. Initially, most of the report portal is empty since we are yet to set up and create the virtual infrastructure. It will take at least a day or two after the complete virtualization infrastructure setup to view various resources and generate reports.

> To learn more about using and gathering reports using the report portal, please refer to *Reports, History Database Reports, and Dashboards* at `https://access.redhat.com/documentation/ en-US/Red_Hat_Enterprise_Virtualization/3.3/html/ Administration_Guide/chap-Reports_History_Database_ Reports_and_Dashboards.html`.

Deploying RHEV Hypervisor

Before starting the hypervisor deployment, make sure the required hardware and software prerequisites are met as mentioned in *Chapter 1, An Overview of Red Hat Enterprise Virtualization*.

First of all, you need to get the hypervisor image by performing the following steps:

RHEV-H ships as an ISO image, which is required to deploy and configure hypervisor.

1. To download the hypervisor CD-ROM image, please log in to Red Hat Network at `https://access.redhat.com/downloads/`.
2. Click on the **Download** section and select **Red Hat Enterprise Virtualization**.
3. Download the latest release of the RHEV-H image (for RHEV-M 3.3) from the channel named **Red Hat Enterprise Virtualization Hypervisor** (for the v6 server).
4. Write the downloaded ISO image of RHEV-H on to the optical CD-ROM media.

Installing the hypervisor

There are two methods to install hypervisor: interactive and unattended installation. We are going to use the interactive installation to better understand the different configuration options to set up our first RHEV-H. To start the interactive installation, follow these steps:

1. Boot the hardware with the first boot option enabled as CD-ROM device with hypervisors ISO image.

2. Boot screen splash with automatic boot in 30 seconds with the default kernel parameters. Press any key to modify it.

3. You can select any one of the options shown in the following screenshot that are relevant to your environment since this is our new deployment. Select **Install Or Upgrade** and then press *Enter*.

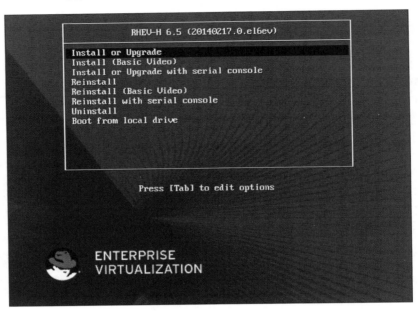

If you get any error such as virtualization extension not enabled, please make sure the virtualization and NX flag are enabled in the system.

4. You can check whether the virtualization and NX flag are enabled from the installer window instead of getting into BIOS by editing **Install or Upgrade**. Press the *Tab* key and then add `rescue` to the kernel parameter and press *Enter*.

5. Once the hypervisor boots, you can verify the CPU virtualization flag by running the following command:

```
# grep -E "svm|vmx" /proc/cpuinfo
```

 You will see some output if the virtualization flag is enabled in your processor. Otherwise, you need to toggle it to ON from your BIOS settings. Please refer to your system manufacturer guide on how to enable the CPU virtualization flag in your system BIOS and continue further.

The output for the preceding command is shown in the following screenshot:

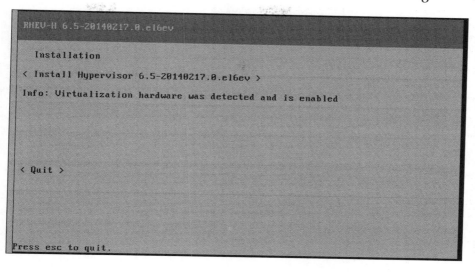

6. After booting your system with hypervisor ISO select **Install or Upgrade** and press *Enter*.

7. Now select the keyboard layouts.

8. Next, the installer will automatically detect all disks attached to the system and give you the option to select the disk to boot.

9. Press *Enter* to select the device. Once the device is selected, click on **Continue** and press *Enter*.

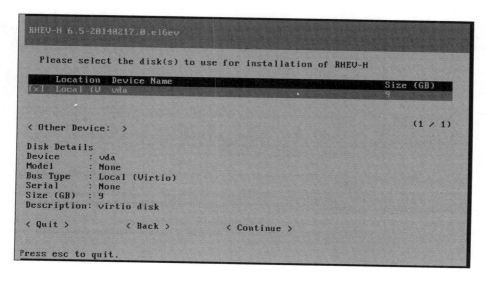

10. This will create the required partition automatically to install and boot the hypervisor image on the selected disk, as shown in the following screenshot:

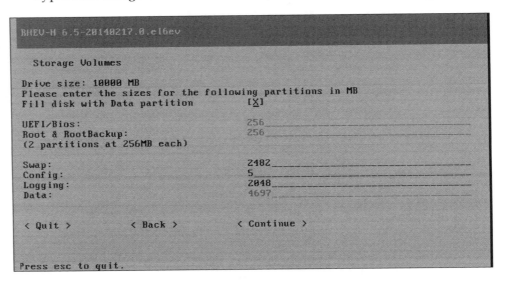

11. Set the password for the admin user and select **Install**. Remember the password as you need this to configure the hypervisor after installation from the admin console.

12. On the next screen, you can see the installation progress status. Once the installation is successful, select **Reboot** and press *Enter*.

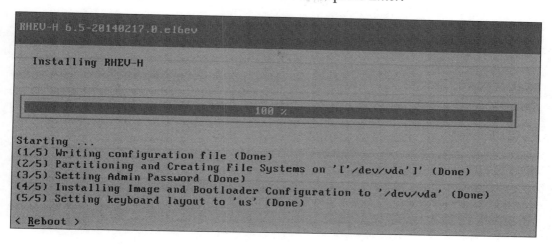

Configuring the hypervisor

After the hypervisor has been installed and rebooted, it will load the admin login console to configure the hypervisor, as shown in the following screenshot:

```
Red Hat Enterprise Virtualization Hypervisor release 6.5 (20140217.0.el6ev)
Kernel 2.6.32-431.5.1.el6.x86_64 on an x86_64 (tty1)

Please login as 'admin' to configure the node
localhost login: admin
Password:
```

Log in as admin with the password we set during the installation. It will take you to the setup screen, as shown here:

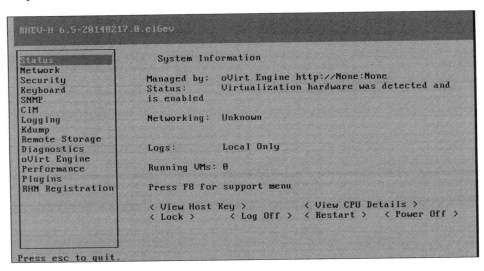

Here, we are going to concentrate only on four sections: **Network, Security, oVirt Engine**, and finally the **Status** tab.

Move to **Network** and set the hostname to `rhev-hypervisor1.example.com`. Configure the DNS server; in our case, it is 192.168.100.84. Set up Network Time Protocol and then click on **Save**, as shown in the following screenshot:

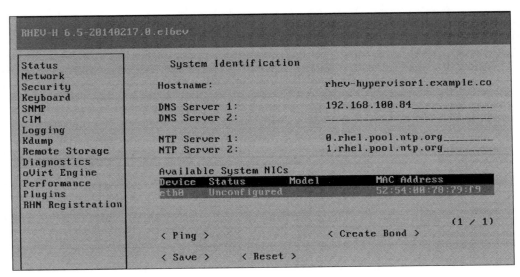

Now, select one of the available NICs and press *Enter*. Configure static networking and populate the VLAN tag if your networking is configured for the VLAN tag. Optionally, select a bridge or leave it unselected and then save, as shown in the following screenshot:

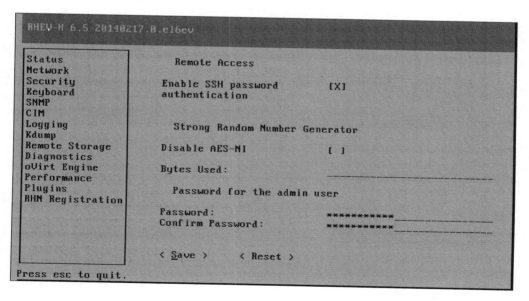

Next, select a ping tab to make sure networking works as expected by running a ping to the RHEV-M machine.

Move to **Security**, enable SSH password authentication for remote access of the hypervisor, and set a password.

Next, move on to the **Ovirt Engine** tab. Under **Management Server**, type in your FQDN of the RHEV-M server; in our case, it is `rhevmanager.example.com`. Leave **Management Server Port** to the default of **443**. Now click on **Retrieve Certificate** and accept the certificate. Finally, click on **Save & Register**, as shown in the following screenshot:

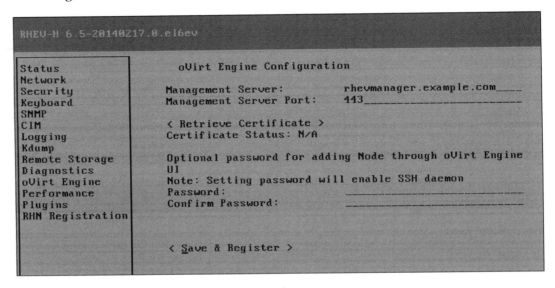

If everything is configured properly, then it activates the VDSM service on its own with a message saying all changes were applied successfully.

Finally, move to the **Status** tab, which will now be populated with all the values we configured.

Now it's time to log off and move back to the RHEV-M admin portal to approve the host, which will show as pending for approval under the **Host** tab. Don't approve now; before that, we need to set up the virtual data center and cluster. We are going to do this in the next chapter.

To use the RHEL host instead of the RHEV-H image as a hypervisor, please refer to the *Installing Red Hat Enterprise Linux Hosts* section at `https://access.redhat.com/documentation/en-US/Red_Hat_Enterprise_Virtualization/3.3/html-single/Installation_Guide/index.html#Preparing_a_Postgres_Database_Server_for_use_with_Red_Hat_Enterprise_Virtualization_Manager`.

RHEV-H installation supports multiple deployment options, which includes installing from USB, a TFTP/PXE boot, and using the CD-ROM device. Refer to the RHEV installation guide for more detailed information on specific types.

Summary

In this chapter, we discussed setting up our basic virtualization infrastructure, which includes installing RHEV-M and the report server and connecting to various portals such as the admin, user, and report portals. Finally, we deployed our first RHEV-H and configured it to host our virtual machines.

In the next chapter, we will learn how to create a virtual data center and cluster, approve a hypervisor host to a cluster, set up and activate virtual machine data storage, populate ISO to create the virtual machines, and use an export disk to export the virtual machine for backup.

Setting Up the RHEV Virtual Infrastructure

3

Now that we have installed and configured the various **Red Hat Enterprise Virtualization (RHEV)** components, we will move on to setting up the virtualization infrastructure from the Manager admin portal to run your workloads on the RHEV virtual environment. Red Hat Enterprise Virtualization contains various logical components, such as data centers, clusters, hosts, storage, networks, disks, and more, which we are going to cover in detail in the rest of the book. This chapter is very critical as it explains how to set up the overall Red Hat Enterprise Virtualization environment.

In this chapter, we will cover the following topics:

- Configuring RHEV
- Creating data centers
- Creating clusters
- Approving hypervisor hosts
- Configuring logical networks
- Adding various storage domains

Configuring RHEV

Now, log in to the administrator portal and configure your RHEV environment by setting up a data center, cluster, hosts, networks, and storage. By default, the RHEV installer creates a default data center and its storage type with a default cluster. Though the default data center is sufficient for your development or testing purposes, it's strongly recommended to create a new data center and name it something relevant to your location or application services just in case you build a multitenant private cloud using RHEV. This will help you easily find the individual performance data and information relevant to that data center. Once you log in to the admin portal, navigate to the tree pane and click on **Expand All** to view the default logical components created by the installer. You can either use the default data center created by the installer or set up a new data center and cluster and add the hypervisor hosts to further set up your virtual environment. In this chapter, we are going to set up a new environment with new logical components, such as a data center, cluster, and so on to better understand RHEV.

> Please perform the procedure in sequence and don't skip any step.

The RHEV-M admin portal provides the tree mode and flat mode to manage your virtualization resources. The tree mode displays resources in a hierarchical view per data center, from the highest level of the data center down to the individual virtual machine. Working in the tree mode is highly recommended for most operations.

The flat mode allows you to search across data centers or storage domains. It does not limit you to viewing the resources of a single hierarchy. To access the flat mode, click on the **System** item in the tree pane on the left side of the screen, as shown in the following screenshot:

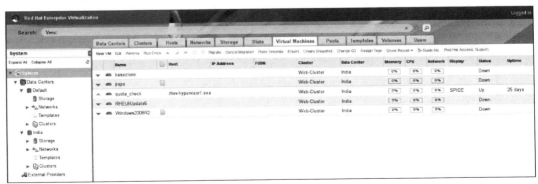

Data centers

A data center is a logical entity that defines the set of physical and logical resources used in a managed virtual environment. Think of it as a container that houses clusters of hosts, virtual machines, storage, and networks. To create a new data center, follow the ensuing steps:

1. Click on the **Data Centers** tab and then on **New**, and give the data center a meaningful name and description.

2. Select iSCSI as **Type** from the drop-down menu and choose **iSCSI (internet Small Computer System Interface)**.

3. Set **Compatibility Version** to **3.3** and leave the **Quota Mode** field set to **Disabled** at this point of time, and we will see how to enable this in our upcoming chapter, which talks about quota management.

4. Finally, provide details in the **Comment** textbox and click on **OK**. Take a look at the following screenshot:

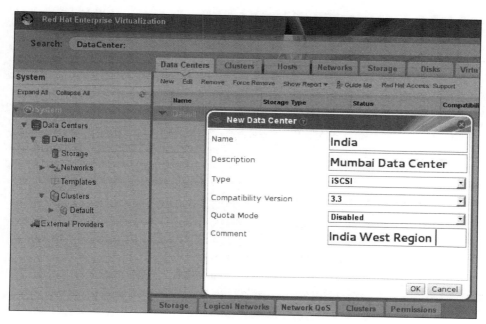

Creating data center

Please pay attention while choosing the storage type of a data center. If you select iSCSI as a storage type, then all the clusters under this data center and the respective hosts will use only the iSCSI storage as a storage domain to store the virtual machine image. Mixing up different storage types in a data center was not supported in RHEV 3.3. But this feature is available from the RHEV 3.4 release.

Once the new data center is created, a **Guide Me** window (shown in the following screenshot) will pop up to guide you further and help you set up your next logical component, that is, a cluster.

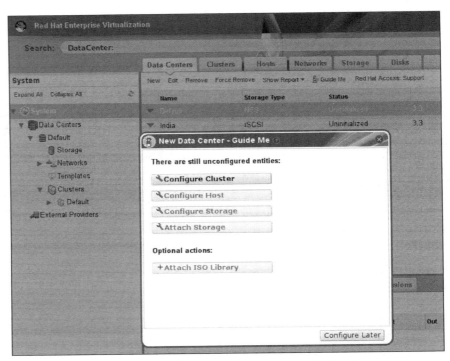

The Guide Me window to set up other components under the data center

Clusters

A cluster is a group of physical hosts that acts as a resource pool for a set of virtual machines created on it. You can create multiple clusters in a data center. For example, you can group a set of hosts and attach them to a cluster named web cluster to run your web server workloads. Similarly, you can group another set of hosts and attach them to a database cluster to run your database workloads. Hosts in the same cluster should share the same CPU, storage types, and network infrastructures. This will allow the live migration of virtual machines across a set of hosts in the same cluster during planned maintenance or while using high availability features of RHEV. To create a new cluster, you have to perform the following steps:

1. Use the **Guide Me** window or navigate to the **Cluster** tab by clicking on the **Configure Later** button of the **Guide Me** window. If you are not using the **Guide Me** window, you need to select the data center on which the cluster is to be created. In this example, we are going to use the **Guide Me** window and select the **Configure Cluster** option.

2. Under the **General** section, give a meaningful name to the cluster along with a description and comment.

3. Select **CPU Name**. Note that it is important to match the CPU processor family to any processor (can be the oldest processor present in any hypervisor in the cluster) you intend to attach to the cluster; otherwise, the host will go into a nonoperational state when you try to activate it. Please refer to your respective CPU vendor guide for more details on Intel and the AMD CPU Family.

4. Set **Compatibility Version** to 3.3 and leave the **Enable Virt Service** radio button checked. You need to check the **Enable Gluster Service** option only when you plan to use the hosts' clusters as gluster storage server nodes and not as running virtual machines.

   Red Hat Storage (RHS), formerly known as GlusterFS, provides a POSIX-compatible filesystem that allows you to store virtual machine images in a Red Hat Storage Server cluster instead of **network-attached storage (NAS)** appliances or a **storage area network (SAN)** array. RedHat Enterprise Virtualization 3.3 and later supports Red Hat Storage as the virtual machine image store. If the RHEV cluster is gluster-enabled, hosts in this cluster will be used as Red Hat Storage Server nodes and not to run virtual machines.

   For more detailed information on using RHS with RHEV, please refer to `https://access.redhat.com/documentation/en-US/Red_Hat_Storage/2.1/html-single/Quick_Start_Guide/index.html#chap-Quick_Start_Guide-Virtual_Intro`.

5. Move to the **Optimization** tab and check the **For Server Load** option to create and manage server class virtual machines, and optionally, you can select the **CPU Threads** and **Memory Ballon** radio buttons as per your requirement. We leave both these radio buttons unchecked in our case.

Please refer to the *Creating a New Cluster* section of the RHEV 3.3 Administrator Guide at `https://access.redhat.com/documentation/ en-US/Red_Hat_Enterprise_Virtualization/3.3/html-single/ Administration_Guide/index.html#Creating_a_New_Cluster` for more detailed information on specific options.

6. Next, select **Resilience Policy** and choose any one of the three options as per your needs. **Resilience Policy** sets the virtual machine migration policy in the event of host failure.

7. Cluster policies will allow you to specify the usage and distribution of virtual machines between available hosts. Define the cluster policy to enable automatic load balancing across the hosts in a cluster. You can select any of the three options as relevant to your environment and workloads. In our example, we will choose the **Even Distribution** cluster policy. Leave **Enable Trusted Service** unchecked (you need this only for integration with the Open Attestation server to manage host integrity in the cloud).

8. Finally, navigate to the **General** tab and click on **OK** to create the cluster. Take a look at the following screenshot:

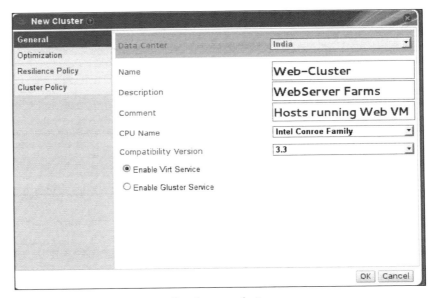

Creating new cluster

Approving hypervisor hosts

We installed and configured RHEV hypervisor hosts and it's shown as waiting for approval under the **Hosts** tab of manager admin portal, as discussed in the *Configuring the Hypervisor* section of *Chapter 2, Installing RHEV Manager and Hypervisor Hosts*. RHEV hypervisor is specifically built for the hypervisor platform and it will come for approval automatically. Now we need to approve the host. You can also configure the hypervisor to add into specific cluster of your data center in RHEV from the **Host** tab manually.

To approve a host, you have to perform the following steps:

1. Navigate to the **Host** tab, select the host, and click on **Approve**.

2. In the **Edit and Approve Host** screen, under the **General** section, select the data center and the host cluster on which this hypervisor host is to be a part of, with some optional comments.

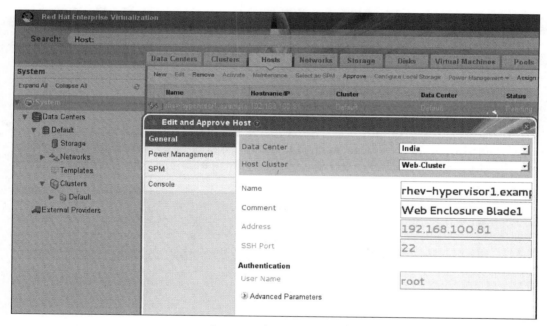

Approving hypervisor host

3. Next, move to the **Power Management** section and select **Enable Power Management** and the type of **Out of Band (OOB)** power management your hardware ships with, and fill in the required server remote management credentials.

    This is mandatory if you are planning to enable high availability of a virtual machine on your environment. For example, say you have two hypervisor hosts running on a cluster. If any of the hosts goes into a nonresponsive state due to some hardware failure, the other active hypervisor will try to recover the host by performing a fence operation (hard reboot) using the server remote management credentials that we have configured, and restart the virtual machines marked **Highly Available** on the other active hosts in the cluster.

4. Then, move to the **SPM** tab. **Storage Pool Manager (SPM)** is a role assigned to one of the hosts in a data center, which will manage and control access to the storage domains. If you have multiple hosts in the cluster or data center, then you can select your preferred host to take over the role of SPM with priority set to low, normal, or high. The SPM role must always be available or the data center will go into a nonresponsive state. Hence, for some reason if one of the SPM hosts fails, the other active hosts in the data center will automatically try to take over the role and bring the data center to the normal up state.

5. **Console Override display address** under the **Console** tab is useful in cases where the hosts are defined by the internal IP address and are behind an NAT firewall. When a user connects to a virtual machine console (using the spice or VNC protocol) from outside the internal network, instead of returning the private address of the host on which the virtual machine is running, a public IP or FQDN (which is resolved in the external network of the public IP) is returned.

6. Move to the **General** tab and click on **OK** to finalize the host approval. Select the **Events** pane at the bottom of the console and expand to see the host approval operations in real time. Refer to the event logs to understand what's going on in the background during the host approval process.

7. The host status will change from **Installing** to **Non Operational** and finally, to **Up**. Take a look at the following screenshot:

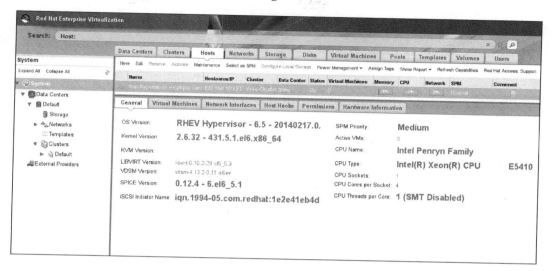

To add the General Purpose Red Hat Enterprise Host as a hypervisor in RHEV, you need a few additional configurations to be made manually post the operating system installation. Please refer to the *Configuring the Hypervisor* section of *Chapter 2, Installing RHEV Manager and Hypervisor Hosts*, to set up and use RHEL host as a hypervisor.

Logical networks

A logical network is mainly used to isolate network traffic by functionalities. You can run your virtual workloads on a host with a single **Network Interface Controller (NIC)**, but it is not recommended to run your mission critical workloads for optimal performance. The following are five different types of network traffic you need to consider during the design phase of RHEV:

- **RHEV-M network**: This is the first logical network created by the RHEV hypervisor installer and attached to the specific NIC of your hypervisor host. It is primarily used for manager and hypervisor heartbeat communication, and also for live migration of virtual machines.

- **Virtual machine networking traffic**: This type of network traffic is primarily used by your application and end user to access the application that runs on the guest.

- **Storage network**: This network is primarily used in a scenario where network storage such as NFS or iSCSI is used as data domains to segregate storage traffic.

- **Live migration traffic**: This type of network traffic allows you to dedicate NIC and attach to the Logical Network for Live Migration traffic of virtual machines across hosts.

- **Display console**: This is used to access the virtual machine console over the network using the spice or VNC protocol for remote administration.

In addition to these networks, other networks can be defined and used to segregate virtual machine traffic from the management networks, or isolate traffic between groups of virtual machines in the same cluster as per the requirement.

The use of VLANs on logical networks also allows a single network interface to be associated with multiple, differently VLAN-tagged logical networks. If VLAN tagging is not used, then each logical network must be associated with one individual physical NIC or bonded device of the hosts. You can't create multiple logical networks on the same NIC.

Adding logical networks

In this section, we are going to learn how we can define a new logical network called vmdata01 in the data center and apply this logical network to the cluster we created, and later attach it to the physical NIC of the approved hosts. To add logical networks, perform the following steps:

1. Navigate to the **Data Centers** tab, click on **Logical Networks** from the bottom pane, and select **New** to create a new logical network.

2. Under the **General** section, fill in the name, description, and comments. And if your host is in a specific VLAN, check **Enable VLAN tagging** and type the VLAN tag ID. Users have to configure their switch port(s) to allow these VLAN tags (refer to the respective vendor switch documentation), or contact the network administrator. Leave **VM Network** selected if you intend to use this logical network for virtual machine traffic.

3. Move to the **Cluster** section, attach the logical network to the cluster we created, and click on **OK**. This will create a new logical network and attach that logical network to the cluster. Take a look at the following screenshot:

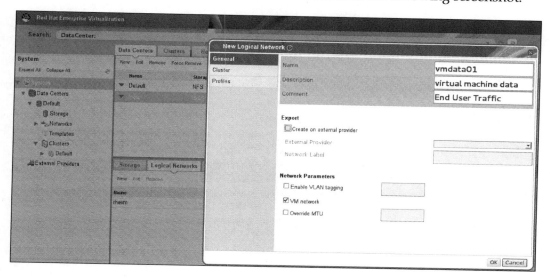

4. Now navigate to the **Cluster** tab, select the cluster you created, and click on **Logical Network**. You will now see a new logical network created in the operational state.

5. Select the logical network and click on **Manage Networks**. You will see a window with the following options:

   ° A checked **Assign All** checkbox for the RHEV-M logical network

   ° A checked **Required All** checkbox for the RHEV-M logical network

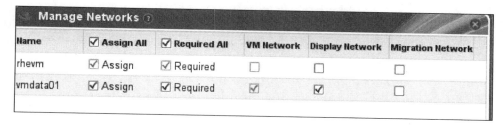

Required networks must be applied to all hosts in a cluster for the cluster and network to be operational. When a required network becomes nonoperational, the virtual machines running on the network are fenced and migrated to another host. This is beneficial if you have machines running on mission critical workloads.

When a non-required network becomes nonoperational, the virtual machines running on the network are not migrated to another host. This prevents unnecessary I/O overload caused by mass migrations.

Optional networks are the logical networks that have not been explicitly declared in the same way as required networks are. Optional networks can be implemented on only the hosts that use them. The presence or absence of these networks does not affect the operational status of a host. Optionally, you can select the logical network used for any of the three functionalities: VM, Display, and Migration Network. Select VM Traffic so that we can use this logical network for all our virtual machine network traffic.

6. Select the option relevant to your requirements and click on **OK**.

Note that you can't edit the RHEV-M logical network. Multiple **Virtual LANs (VLANs)** can be added to a single or bonded network interface to separate traffic based on VLAN.

7. Navigate to the **Host** tab. Select the hosts and click on the **Network Interface** tab.

8. Click on **Set up Host Networks**.

9. Drag your newly created logical network from the left-hand side under the **Assigned Logical Networks** area next to the physical network. In our case, we dragged **vmdata01** and tied it to the physical interface **eth2**. Check the **Save network configuration** checkbox and click on **OK** to finalize the network setup.

10. If everything is configured properly, you will see your new logical network attached to the physical NIC, and the interface status changes from the **Down** state to the **Up** state under the **Network Interfaces** tab of the hosts, as shown in the following screenshot:

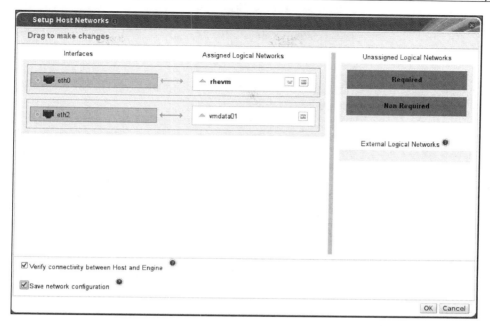

11. If you have multiple network devices on hypervisor hosts, you can bond compatible network devices together to increase the available network bandwidth and reliability. To set up network bonding and understand the supported bonding logic and modes in RHEV, please refer to the *Hosts and Networking* section of the RHEV 3.3 Administration Guide at `https://access.redhat.com/documentation/en-US/Red_Hat_Enterprise_Virtualization/3.3/html-single/Administration_Guide/index.html#sect-Hosts_and_Networking`.

Storage domains

RHEV supports multiple storage types, such as FC, iSCSI, NFS, local storage, POSIX Complaint, and Gluster File System. Note that you can't mix up different storage types in a data center on RHEV 3.3. In RHEV, there are three different storage domains:

- **Data domain**: This is used to store the virtual machines' images, snapshots, and templates

- **ISO domain**: This is used to store the operating system library for virtual machine deployment as well as the virtual floppy drive

- **Export/Import domain**: This is used to back up all your virtual machine images and use the same disk as an import domain to move your virtual workloads across the data centers in the same or other RHEV environments

In this guide, we are going to use the storage type of iSCSI for our data storage domains, and NFS disks for ISO and export/import domains. Please refer to *Chapter 10, Setting Up iSCSI, NFS, and IdM Directory Services for RHEV*, to set up your own NFS and iSCSI server on RHEL to serve ISO, export storage domain, and data storage domains for your RHEV infrastructure.

Adding a data domain to store virtual machines

After the first hypervisor is approved and registered to the cluster, you will still see that the data center status is in the uninitialized state. To initialize the data center, we need to perform the last and most important setup of adding the storage domain to store the virtual machines' images. In this guide, we are going to use the storage type of iSCSI for our first data storage domain, and attach it to the new data center with the storage type of iSCSI, which we created earlier in this chapter. Perform the following steps to add a data domain to store virtual machines:

1. If you are using any type of network storage like NFS or iSCSI as a data domain, it's highly recommended to dedicate a network interface on hypervisors' hosts to access the network storage so that all the storage traffic will get isolated from the end user traffic accessing the application hosted on your virtual machines. To add an iSCSI storage domain, navigate to the **Storage** tab after you have logged in to the administrator portal and click on **New Domain**.

2. Give a meaningful name to the data domain, select the data center from the drop-down menu, change **Domain Function / Storage Type** to **Data / ISCSI**, and leave the **Format V3** unchanged.

3. Under the **Use Host** drop-down menu, select the host you want to perform an initial storage configuration for. Note that only the hosts registered to the data center will only be displayed under the drop-down menu.

4. Then, under the **Discover Targets** section, fill in your iSCSI server FQDN in the **Address** textbox, select **Port**, check the **User Authentication** option, and fill in the chap login credentials, if in case your iSCSI storage server is enabled with authentication to restrict iSCSI access to storage volumes.

5. Finally, click on **Discover**, which will instruct the host that you selected to discover the iSCSI target and returns with all the target names that are exported from your iSCSI server to this host. Select the target and click on **Login**.

6. Once the host is logged in to the iSCSI, target the same screen and you will get an option to expand the target name in order to select the LUN you want to use for this data domain. Select the LUN and click on the **OK** button. Take a look at the following screenshot:

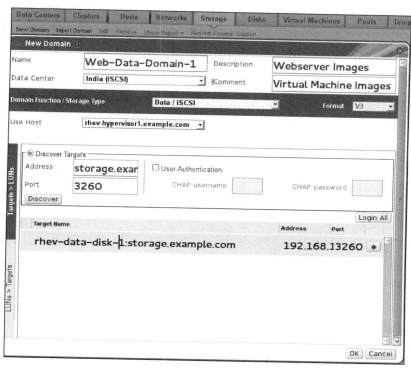

Adding the ISCSI data domain

After a few seconds, the new storage domain we created will get attached to the data center we created, go into the locked state, and return automatically to the active state. Wait till the first data domain turns to the up state before you proceed further. You can see that the new data domain holds the status of **Master**, which is used to store the metadata of storage domains, handle cluster locks, handle creation and deletion of virtual machine images, and manage SPM leases. The **Master** data domain role can migrate across any active storage domains in the data center as per the need.

Adding a data domain of other storage types

Please note that creating a data storage domain using the storage type of iSCSI and FCP are mostly similar except under FCP there is no need to enter any discovery target section, where selecting the host will automatically scan for the LUN presented to the host via a fiber channel.

If you plan to use NFS as a data storage domain, then please refer to the *Configuring and activating export domain* section of this chapter where we are going to use NFS exports as backend storage for the export and import of virtual machines. The only difference is that you need to follow the same step, except the **Domain / Storage Type** should be changed to **Data / NFS** instead of **Export / NFS** while adding the NFS disk as a data domain.

Activating the ISO domain

You have now created an iSCSI storage data domain. Now, you need to attach an ISO domain to the data center and upload installation images so that you can use them to create virtual machines. Before that, if you recollect, we had already created an ISO domain during the RHEV-M engine-setup installation and chose /rhev-iso-library as a destination on Manager Box to store the ISO library.

For this reason, under the **Storage** tab, you can see the ISO_Datastore of the storage type ISO display with the status **Unattached**. To attach the ISO Domain to a data center, perform the following steps:

1. Go to the **Storage** tab, select the ISO datastore, select **Data center** on the bottom pane and click on **Attach**.

2. You will see a pop-up window with a list of the active data centers in your setup to attach this ISO domain. Select the appropriate data center and click on **OK**. This will attach the ISO datastore to the data center you selected and change its status to the **Inactive** state for a couple of seconds and turns to the **Active** state on its own.

Now we have two data domains in the **Active** state in our data center: one to store the virtual machine and another to store the ISO library. Please note that in a data center at least one data domain should be in the active state before attaching and activating the ISO domain. Also, you can move the ISO storage domain to multiple data centers in your RHEV environment to create virtual machines.

Populate ISO images on an ISO domain

To install a virtual machine or run live boot images such as a backup appliance, media images (CD-ROM or DVD-ROM in the form of ISO images) must be available in the ISO repository for the virtual machines to use. To do so, RHEV provides a utility that copies the images and sets the appropriate permissions on the file. The file provided to the utility and the ISO share has to be accessible from the RHEV Manager server. Perform the following steps to populate ISO images on the ISO domain:

1. Log in to the RHEV-M server using SSH and make sure you have access to ISO images as well as the ISO library destination before you start uploading. In our guide, we use the `/rhev-iso-library` folder of the RHEV Manager server to store the ISO library, and we also download the RHEL version 6 update 5 ISO image and keep it under the `/opt` directory on the same RHEV Manager server.

2. Now, find out about the active ISO library by running the following command after you've logged in as root on the manager box. The following command will prompt you for the admin password of the manager, which you will need to provide:

    ```
    [root@rhevmanager ~]# engine-iso-uploader  list
    Please provide the REST API password for the admin@internal oVirt
    Engine user (CTRL+D to abort):
    ISO Storage Domain Name   | Datacenter              | ISO Domain
    Status
    ISO_Datastore             | India                   | active
    [root@rhevmanager ~]#
    ```

3. Now, we have all the information to upload the ISO image. So, to upload the image, run the following command:

    ```
    [root@rhevmanager ~]# engine-iso-uploader -v upload  -i ISO_
    Datastore /opt/rhel-server-6.5-x86_64-dvd.iso
    Please provide the REST API password for the admin@internal oVirt
    Engine user (CTRL+D to abort):
    ```

4. Run `engine-iso-uploader -h` for more help and various options. Be patient; uploading is time-consuming and depends on your storage performance.

5. After the ISO image from RHEV-M has been uploaded, cross-check the upload from the RHEV-M administrator portal or run the `engine-iso-uploader list` command from the manager system.

6. To check the ISO image from the Manager admin console, move on to the **Storage** tab, select the ISO datastore, and click on the **Images** tab on the bottom pane. You will see the ISO image that was recently uploaded to the ISO domain. If it is not visible, please click on the refresh icon at the corner of the screen.

Configuring and activating an export domain

An export storage domain can be attached to a data center to enable the import or export of virtual machines from one data center to another. It can also be used to back up virtual machines and templates. Please note that the export domain will be attached only to a single data center at a given time. Follow the ensuing steps to add a fresh new export domain to your RHEV data center:

1. Go to the **Storage** tab, click on **New Domain**, and give a descriptive name to the export domain. Select the data center and host.

2. Select the **Domain Function / Storage Type** as **Export / NFS**.

3. Leave the rest as default and under the **Export Path** section, enter your NFS storage server FQDN followed by the export path of the export disk. For example, in our case, the export path looks like `storage.example.com:/export/rhev_import_export_disk`. Click on **OK**. Refer to the following screenshot:

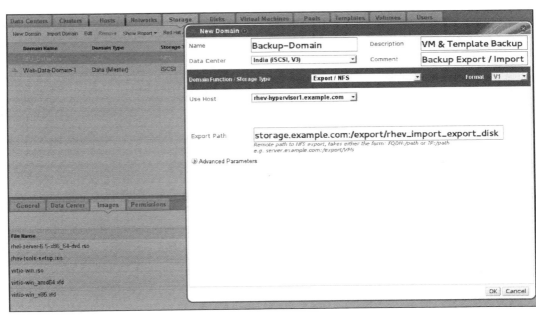

4. Now, the export disk will start to show up in an unattached state for some time before coming to the active state on its own.

5. Also, you might notice an option called **Import Domain** under the **Storage** tab; you need to use this to move your export domain, which was configured earlier, or ISO domain across multiple data centers in the RHEV.

So, we now have three storage domains attached and activated on our RHEV data center. One is of the **Data** type to store virtual machine images, the second is to store ISO, and the third is to export and import virtual machines and templates across data centers. And the stage is set to create and manage your first virtual machine on your RHEV infrastructure, which we are going to see in detail in the next chapter.

Summary

In this chapter, we discussed setting up various logical components such as data centers, and clusters, registering a hypervisor host to a cluster, cluster policies for high availability, setting up logical networks for end user traffic to access the application hosted on virtual machines, various configured and activated storage domain types to store virtual machine images, and backing up those images to restore or move them to other RHEV data centers.

In the next chapter, we will see how to create your first virtual machine on the RHEV infrastructure and templates from the virtual machines as golden images that can be reused. Later, we will see how to clone a virtual machine from the templates and take live virtual machine snapshots, which will be useful in a scenario prior to applying patches to your critical production workloads. Finally, we will see how to back up complete virtual machine images into an export domain to be reused later, or move them to other RHEV environments or across data centers.

4
Creating and Managing Virtual Machines

So far, we have configured the entire required virtualization environment in order to create your virtual machines on RHEV. In this chapter, will learn how to create Red Hat Enterprise Linux and Windows virtual machines from scratch on the RHEV infrastructure and guest agents' installation to enhance the performance. Also, we will learn how to create virtual machine templates so that you can use these templates to rapidly create a replica of the original virtual machine, how to take virtual machine snapshots, and how to restore the virtual machine from these snapshots. In the final section of this chapter, we will learn how to back up your virtual machine using the export disks to move your virtual workloads from one data center to another in the same, as well as the new, RHEV environment. We will cover the following topics in this chapter:

- Virtual machines
- Creating Linux virtual machines
- Creating Windows virtual machines
- Virtual machine templates
- Creating Linux virtual machine templates
- Creating Windows virtual machine templates
- Using templates to create virtual machines
- Virtual machine snapshots
- Creating and restoring virtual machine snapshots
- Backing up your virtual machine to export domains

Virtual machines

A virtual machine is a software implementation of a machine such as your physical hardware that executes programs like a physical machine. It runs its own operating system and allows you to host your application on it. Like physical hardware, the virtual machine uses virtual devices such as virtual hard drives, CPUs, network adapters, memory, and other hardware resources that are managed by a virtualization layer, in our case, KVM. KVM translates all these virtual resource requests to the physical hardware where the virtual machine is hosted.

Creating Linux virtual machines

On RHEV, you can create a virtual machine from existing virtual machine templates or from scratch. Since this is our fresh deployment, we are going to learn how to create a virtual machine from scratch, and then in later sections of the chapter, we are going to learn how to create a virtual machine template and clone a virtual machine using these templates.

General settings

To install a RHEL v6 virtual machine, perform the following steps:

1. Once you log in to **Administrator Portal**, navigate to the **Virtual Machines** tab, and click on **New VM**.

2. In the **New Virtual Machine Creation** windows, fill in all the required fields.

3. In the **General** tab, select the cluster on which you want to run this virtual machine.

4. Leave **Based on Template** as **Blank**. Templates are nothing but master copies of an already created virtual machine with an installed operating system, software packages, and predefined configuration settings such as the security policy and more. We need to use this once the virtual machine template has been created for the mass deployment of identical virtual machines using the existing template.

5. For the **Operating system** field, select **Red Hat Enterprise Linux 6 x.64**. Other Linux operating systems such as Fedora, SUSE, and Ubuntu can be virtualized, but there is a limitation to the Red Hat support for these distributions.

> Please refer to the *Supported Virtual Machine Operating Systems* section in Administration Guide for detailed information at `https://access.redhat.com/documentation/en-US/Red_Hat_Enterprise_Virtualization/3.3/html/Administration_Guide/Supported_virtual_machines.html`.

6. In the **Optimized for** field's drop-down menu, you will find the **Server** and **Desktop** options; select **Server Workload**, give a relevant name to the virtual machine under the **Name** field, and give a meaningful description and comment in the **Description** and **Comment** fields, respectively.

7. Select **Stateless** if you want to run your virtual machine in the stateless mode.

    This is useful only for the desktop workload intended for short-time access by temporary staff. **Stateless** will remove all the data stored by the user on the operating system when the virtual machine reboots.

    The **Start in Pause Mode** option will allow you to establish a SPICE connection over a slow WAN connectivity, which requires a long time to establish a SPICE or VNC connection to a virtual machine.

    The **Delete Protection** option will enable you to protect a virtual machine from accidental deletion. If this option is checked, you have to uncheck this box before deleting the virtual machine.

8. Assign a network interface by selecting a drop-down menu, and choose the relevant profile. In our case, we used **Silver/vmdata01**. If you want to add more interfaces, use the plus sign (+), and to remove it, use the minus sign.

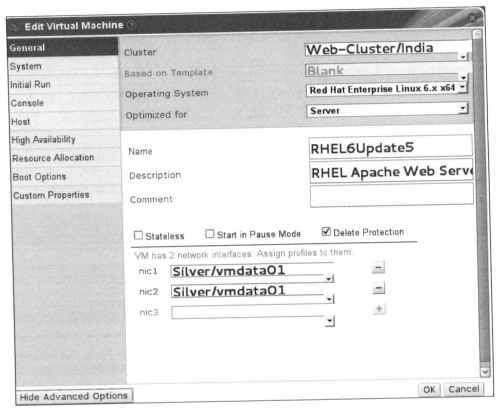

9. Move to the **Console** tab on the left-hand side of the window, and leave all the values to default. If you are creating a desktop workload and are in need of multiple monitors, please select the value from the drop-down menu of **Monitors**.

10. Click on the **Show Advanced Options** tab in the lower-left corner of the window; this will display a list of other advanced settings that are used to configure a given virtual machine, as shown in the upcoming screenshots.

System settings

The **System** settings can be performed using the following steps:

1. Move to **System,** and then allocate the memory size and virtual CPU.

2. Expand **Advanced Parameters** and customize the **Cores per Virtual Socket** and **Virtual Sockets** fields as per your application and its licensing requirement.

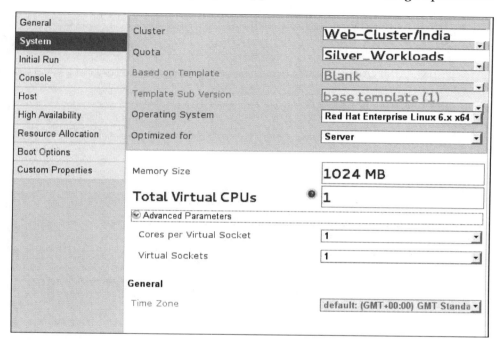

Initial Run settings

The **Initial Run** settings can be performed using the following steps:

1. Move to the **Initial Run** tab in order to join the virtual machine to a domain during the initial run. This option is enabled only if you select the **Operating System** type as **Windows** in the **General** section.

2. Select the **Time Zone** option and fill in the domain details if you want the Windows virtual machine to join the domain during the initial run. The **Domain** field is populated with a list of domains only if you have integrated your RHEV-M with domain controllers.

Console settings

The Console settings can be performed using the following steps:

1. In the **Console** tab, under the **Protocol** section, select either **SPICE** or **VNC** as a display protocol in order to connect to your virtual machine console in the same way as you would use a physical desktop.

2. SPICE is recommended for both Linux and Windows virtual desktop workloads except Windows 8 and 2012. VNC is highly recommended for the server class guest operating system because of its cross-platform, lightweight, and low bandwidth with compression, and it can be encrypted over SSH. If you select **VNC**, select the appropriate **VNC Keyboard Layout** option. Keep in mind that if you select **VNC**, you need a VNC client to connect to the virtual machine console.

3. The **USB Support** option is available only if you select **SPICE** as a protocol; you can choose to either enable or disable this option. If you enable **USB Support**, it will allow you to pass through USB devices from your thin client or desktop to the virtual machine. You can choose either one of the following three options to enable the USB support:

    ○   **Native**: This supports both Linux and Windows workloads and does not require any in-guest agents to be installed on virtual machines. This is supported only for virtual machines running on clusters with the compatibility version set to 3.1 or higher.

    ○   **Legacy**: This is supported only for Windows guests running on RHEV 3.0, and it's going to be depreciated in future releases.

    ○   **Disabled**: This does not allow USB redirection from the client machine to the virtual machine. Select or unselect the **Smartcard Enabled** checkbox to activate or deactivate the smartcard authentication for individual virtual machines.

4. Expand the **Advanced Parameters** option, and you will see **Disable strict user checking** by default.

    This option is enabled by default, which will allow only one user to connect to the console of a virtual machine; the exception is a super user. The new user can connect to the same virtual machine console only after the virtual machine gets rebooted. If you disable this, then you can expose the previous user's session to the new user. Leave this to default.

    The **Soundcard enabled** option is recommended only for desktop workloads; leave it disabled for server class machines.

5. Select the **VirtIO Console Device Enabled** checkbox to attach a VirtIO console device to your virtual machine.

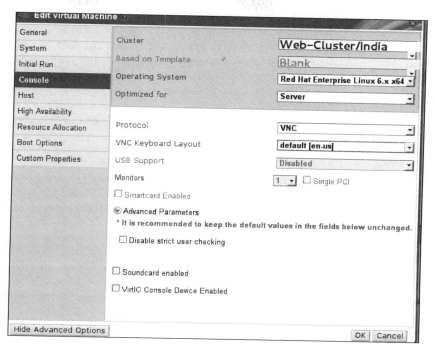

For more information, please refer to the *Virtual Machine Console Settings Explained* section (section 8.4.3.4) explained in the Administration Guide available at `https://access.redhat.com/documentation/en-US/Red_Hat_Enterprise_Virtualization/3.3/html/Administration_Guide/Virtual_Machine_Console_settings_explained.html`.

Host settings

The **Host** settings can be performed using the following steps:

1. Under the **Host** setting tab, you can choose to run the virtual machine on any host in the cluster or pin it to a specific host in the cluster by choosing the **Any Host in Cluster** or **Specific** options, respectively. If you choose **Specific**, then you can select a host from the drop-down box.

   This will enable the virtual machine to start only on this host, and later, the administrator will migrate the virtual machine to other hosts in the cluster depending upon the migration policy setting, as explained in the next step.

2. Under the **Migration Options** setting, you can choose any of the three options:

   ○ **Allow Manual and automatic migration**: This will enable auto live migration depending upon the cluster policy we defined while creating the cluster, and it will also allow the administrator to manually migrate the virtual machine to other hosts in the cluster.

   ○ **Allow manual migration only**: This option doesn't allow the automatic live migration but only allows manual migration by the administrator.

   ○ **Do not allow migration**: The virtual machine cannot be migrated either automatically or manually.

   Use Host CPU: This will allow virtual machines to take advantage of the features of the physical CPU of the host on which it's running. You need to choose **Do not allow migration** to enable this option. The available options for the **Host** section are shown in the following screenshot:

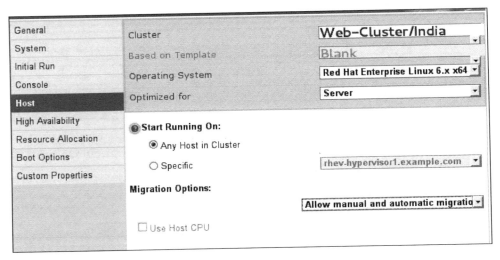

 If you enable **Do not allow migration** under the **Host** setting, it will prevent you from enabling the virtual machine **High Availability** and its priority.

High Availability settings

Move to the **High Availability** settings to define the following high availability features for a virtual machine:

- **Priority for Run/Migration queue**: This sets the priority level for the virtual machine to be migrated or restarted on another host.

- **Watchdog**: This is a timer that is used to automatically detect and recover from failures and is especially useful for servers that demand high availability. You can attach a watchdog card to a virtual machine. The only supported model that you can choose from the drop-down menu at the time of writing this book is **i6300esb**.

  You can also configure what action is to be performed from the drop-down menu if a virtual machine failure is detected by the watchdog. For more information on using watchdog, please refer to the *Virtual Machine High Availability Settings Explained* section in the *Creating Virtual Machine* section of RHEV Administration Guide available at `https://access.redhat.com/documentation/en-US/Red_Hat_Enterprise_Virtualization/3.3/html/Administration_Guide/Virtual_Machine_High_Availability_settings_explained.html`.

To make the virtual machine highly available, check the **Highly Available** option, as shown in the following screenshot:

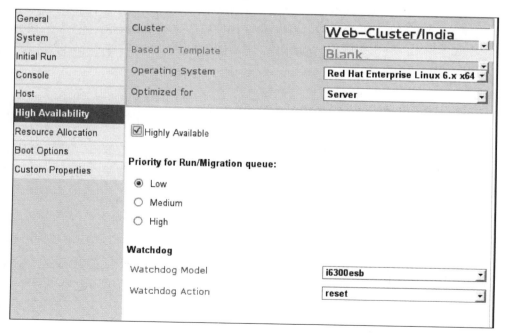

Resource Allocation settings

The **Resource Allocation** tab allows you to define the following compute resource settings for a virtual machine:

- **CPU Shares**: Under the **CPU Allocation** section, you can enable **CPU Shares** and define the CPU share value to a predefined or custom level. This option allows users to specify the priority of CPU utilization among virtual machines with shared CPU resources. A virtual machine marked with a **High** priority will receive twice the amount of CPU resources allocated to the **Medium** priority machines and four times the amount allocated to a **Low** priority machine.

- **CPU Pinning topology**: This enables the virtual machine's virtual CPU to run on a specific **physical CPU (pCPU)** in a specific host. This option is enabled only if you choose **Do not allow migration** under the **Host** setting of the virtual machine creation.

- **Physical Memory Guaranteed**: This is the amount of physical memory guaranteed for the virtual machine, and you can customize it as per your requirements.

- **Memory Balloon Device Enabled**: This checkbox enables memory overcommit on virtual machines. When this option is set, the **Memory Overcommit Manager (MoM)** will start ballooning where and when possible with a limitation on the guaranteed memory size of every virtual machine.

- **Storage Allocation**: This is available only when a template is selected. We will see this in detail when creating the virtual machine from the templates later in the chapter.

VirtIO-SCSI Enabled: This will allow you to attach the VirtIO SCSI controller when running the virtual machine. The available options for the **Resource Allocation** section are shown in the following screenshot:

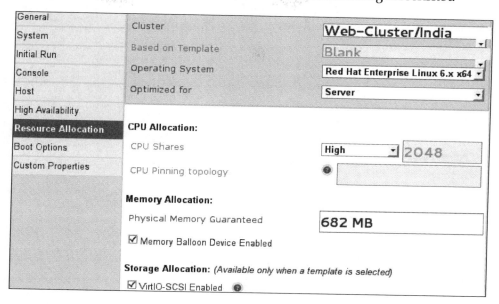

Boot Options settings

The **Boot Options** settings can be performed using the following steps:

1. Navigate to **Boot Options** to set the boot parameters for a virtual machine.

2. Select the **First Device** and **Second Device** options for your virtual machine to boot post the operating system installation.

3. The **Attach CD** checkbox will allow you to choose the `.iso` images from drop-down menu for the operating system installation. Keep in mind that the ISO must be uploaded and be visible in the ISO domain.

To attach the Red Hat Enterprise Linux ISO image, check the **Attach CD** button, as shown in the following screenshot, and select the respective ISO image:

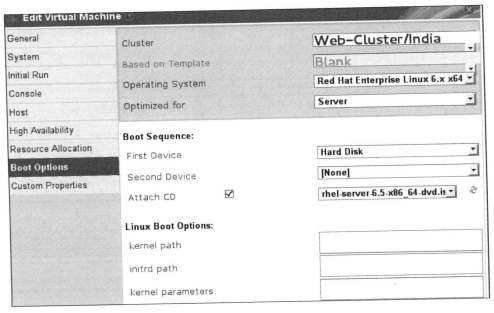

Custom Properties

The **Custom Properties** settings can be performed using the following steps:

1. The **Custom Properties** section will allow you to choose any four of the predefined features from the drop-down menu.

2. Review all of your settings and click on **OK**.

Adding virtual disks

After we reviewed and confirmed the virtual machine settings in the previous **Boot Options** section, a new virtual machine's **Guide Me** window opens, and this will allow you to add storage disks to the virtual machine.

To add a virtual hard disk to the virtual machine, perform the following steps:

1. Click on **Configure Virtual Disks** to add storage to the virtual machine.

2. Enter a value in the **Size** field of the disk with a description on what that disk is used for in the **Description** field.

3. Select **VirtIO** as **Interface**.

   VirtIO is highly recommended for better performance. RHEL 5 and later releases ship VirtIO drivers in the kernel itself. For Windows workloads, you can attach the virtual floppy drive while starting the operating system installation using the **Run Once** option. The virtual floppy drive contains all the required VirtIO drivers that detect the virtual hard drive by the operating system installer in order to proceed to the Windows operating system installation for bootable disks. Post the Windows operating system installation, you can attach guest tools to the virtual machine as a CD-ROM device and install the required guest drivers for the network adapter. For more detailed information using the VirtIO on Windows guest operating system, please refer to the *Installing VirtIO drivers during a Windows installation* section in this chapter.

4. Under the **Allocation Policy** field, select **Preallocated**.

   The **Preallocated** option allots the entire size of the disk on the data domain at the time of creation. This is highly recommended for server and disk I/O intensive workloads. The creation of preallocated disks takes some time, and it highly depends upon the size of your virtual hard disk. Thin provisioned disks are faster to create and allow for storage overcommit. Thin provisioned disks are recommended for desktop disks only.

5. For the **Storage Domain** dropdown, select the storage domain from which you want to create and attach the virtual disk for your virtual machine.

6. The **Wipe After Delete** checkbox provides you with enhanced security for the deletion of sensitive material when the disk is deleted.

7. Check the **Is Bootable** option for your first virtual drive to install the operating system on it. This will set the bootable flag on the disk. It's possible to add only one bootable disk to the guest operating system. Check the **Is Shareable** option if you want to share and attach the disk to more than one virtual machine at a time.

   It's useful to create a high-availability guest cluster between the sets of virtual machines to access the shared storage of data. To efficiently use sharing disks across multiple virtual machines, you need some cluster-aware software to run on these guests, which will take care of simultaneous read/write operations of the disks across these guests in order to avoid any filesystem corruption. For more details on shareable disks, please refer to the *Shareable Disks* section in *Chapter 6, Advanced Storage and Networking Features*.

8. Finally, click on **OK**, and the window will pop up with an option to add a second drive. Then, click on **Configure later**. The virtual machine will momentarily go into the locked state while attaching the virtual hard disk before coming back to the down state.

The following screenshot explains the various settings we discussed in the preceding section:

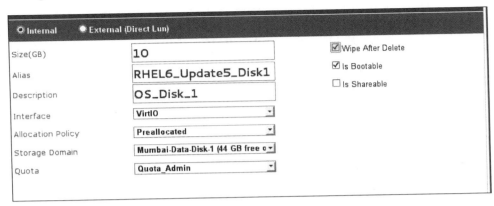

Installing Red Hat Enterprise Linux on a virtual machine

Before you start the guest operation deployment in order to connect to a graphical console of a virtual machine that proceeds to the installation, you need a few console-supported components installed on your client machine from where you are going to access and create a new virtual machine from the administration portal.

For clients running Mozilla Firefox on Linux systems, the SPICE plugin is required to run a SPICE client remote viewer application in order to access the virtual machine's graphical console. To install the SPICE client, log in to the client as a root, and from the terminal, install the SPICE and virt-viewer packages using the following command:

```
#yum install spice-xpi virt-viewer
```

Once this is installed, restart Mozilla Firefox in order to connect to your virtual machines using SPICE.

On Windows, the client's SPICE ActiveX component is required to connect to a virtual machine console. When you access the virtual machine console for the first time from the supported **Internet Explorer** (**IE**) running on your Windows client, IE will prompt you to download and install the SPICE ActiveX component. Follow the onscreen instructions and confirm the security warning to complete the installation.

Finally, restart IE to connect to your virtual machines using SPICE.

Once you configure the required resource in order to run virtual machine and graphical console access from your client machine, it's time to the install the operating system on these virtual machines.

To install the RHEL guest operating system, use the following steps:

1. Select your virtual machine and right click on it to select **Run Once**.

2. In the pop-up window, expand **Boot Options** and select the .iso image from the **Attach CD** drop-down menu.

3. Optionally, you can customize **Linux Boot Options** to boot a Linux kernel directly instead of booting it through the BIOS boot loader for the custom kick-start-based Linux installation.

4. The **Initial Run** section will allow you to enable cloud-init, which will allow you to automate various functions such as the hostname, networking, and root password during the initial setup of the virtual machine. This will be quite handy if you derive a new virtual machine from the existing virtual machine template in order to prevent any network conflicts.

 To automate the initial configuration of a Linux virtual machine that has been provisioned based on a template using cloud-init, you need to install a package named cloud-init.

5. The **Host** section will further allow you to customize where you want to start this guest. Also, there is an optional **Display Protocol** modification section and the **Custom Properties** section.

6. After selecting all the required options, click on **Ok** to start the virtual machine. Select your virtual machine, and right-click on it to select **Console**.

   This displays a window to the virtual machine where you will be prompted to start installing the operating system. For further instructions, please refer to Red Hat Enterprise Linux Installation Guide available at https:// access.redhat.com/documentation/en-US/Red_Hat_Enterprise_ Linux/6/html/Installation_Guide/.

The following screenshot explains the various settings we discussed in the preceding section on using **Run Once** to start the operating system installation:

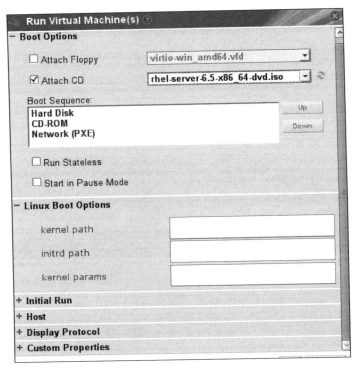

After the installation is complete, shut down the virtual machine and reboot the hard drive. You can now connect to your RHEL virtual machine and start using it to deploy your application for the end user access.

Installing guest agents and drivers on RHEL guests

The RHEV guest agent and drivers for Linux and Windows guests improve overall guests' performance and allow RHEV-M to show the memory, CPU, network utilization, IP address of the virtual machine, installed application of these virtual machines, enable **Single Sign-On (SSO)**, and more.

To install the guest agent on your RHEL virtual machine, subscribe your guest operating system to the Red Hat Enterprise Virt Agent channel of Red Hat Network.

For RHEL 5 guests, you need to subscribe to the channel named `rhel-x86_64-rhev-agent-5-server`, and for RHEL 6 guests, you need to use the channel labeled `rhel-x86_64-rhev-agent-6-server`.

Once you have subscribed to the relevant channel, run the following command to install the guest agent on your virtual machine. Once it's installed, you can start the guest agent by calling the `init` script of the oVirt-guest-agent:

```
# yum install rhevm-guest-agent
# /etc/init.d/ovirt-guest-agent start
```

Once the RHEL guest agent is installed successfully, you can view the list of installed applications under the **Virtual Machines** tab of your manager for the selected virtual machine by navigating to the **Applications** tab on the bottom pane. Also, this will list the virtual machine IP address that is configured and active on the virtual machine.

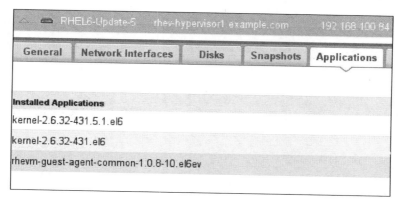

You need to register your RHEL guest to its base channel in Red Hat Network before subscribing to the child channel. Please refer to the Red Hat installation guide on how to subscribe your system to various software channels in Red Hat Network. Also, refer to the earlier chapters where we registered the manager system to Red Hat Network.

Creating Windows virtual machines

To create a Windows Server class virtual machine, you need to follow the same steps as the ones outlined for the Red Hat Enterprise virtual machine.

In this section, we are going to learn how to deploy a Windows 2008 R2 64 Bit Server operating system as a guest operating system:

1. Click on **Create New virtual machine** under the **Virtual Machines** tab.

   Follow the same steps as the ones outlined for the RHEV machine creation. There is only a slight change—explained as follows—that you need to take care of before creating the Windows guest and during the Windows operating system installation.

2. Under the **General** virtual machine creation window, select the **Show Advanced** option.

3. In the **Initial Run** screen, you will get an option to set the time zone of the guest and domain to be joined.

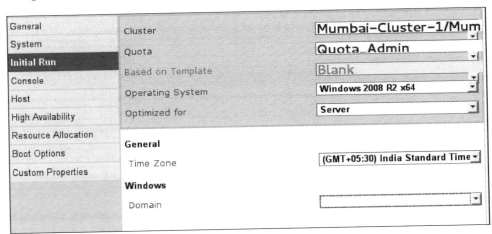

 For the domains to be visible under the drop-down menu, you must integrate RHEV-M with the respective domain controllers in your environment in advance. We are going to see the integration of RHEV-M with other directory services in *Chapter 7, Quota and User Management*.

Installing VirtIO drivers during the Windows installation

The Windows installer doesn't ship any VirtIO drivers as a part of the operating system installer. If you remember, we mentioned using the virtual hard drive interface type in order to set it to VirtIO for better I/O performance in the *Adding virtual disk* section in this chapter. So, if you attach a virtual hard disk type of VirtIO and try to boot your Windows installer, the installer will not able to detect your virtual hard drive. To overcome this, we need to use a virtual floppy drive uploaded automatically by the RHEV-M installer under the ISO domain. To install the VirtIO driver before starting the Windows operating system installation, follow these steps:

1. Go to the **Images** tab of **ISO Storage domain**, and you will see the list of prepopulated guest drivers' ISO and virtual floppy drives.

2. Once you have configured all the required resources for the virtual machine to start, select the virtual machine, and right-click on it to select **Run Once**.

3. In the **Run Once** window, under **Boot Options**, select **Attach Floppy** and the virtual floppy drive, which is **virtio-win_amd64.vfd**, since we are going to deploy the 64-bit edition of the Windows guest operating system. Though the virtual floppy's `.vfd` file ends with `amd64`, the same file should be used for both Intel and AMD x86_64-bit machines. In the **Attach CD** field, select the appropriate Windows ISO for installation.

4. Under the **Initial Run** section of the **Run Once** window, you can use the **Sysprep** utility to automate your Windows guest installation. To enable Sysprep, attach the Sysprep floppy from the **Attach Floppy** drop-down menu.

5. The rest of the options are intact, such as the Linux virtual machine creation, so move ahead and click on **OK**.

6. Select the virtual machine, right-click on it, and select **Console**. This displays a window to the virtual machine where you will be prompted to begin installing the operating system.

7. Windows installations include an option to load additional drivers early in the installation process. Use the **Load drivers** option and then use **Browse**; this will list your **Floppy drive(A:)** attached to the virtual machine. Expand it, select **amd64** and the operating system version, and release it — in our case, this is **win2008R2** — and hit *Enter*.

8. This will give you the option to install three VirtIO drivers, one for the virtual Ethernet adapter, SCSI controller, and SCSI pass-through controller. Select **SCSI controller** and press *Enter*; this will install the necessary VirtIO driver, and your virtual hard drive will get detected to proceed with the installation of the Windows operating system. For further instructions, please refer to Windows 2008 R2 Installation Guide available at `http://technet.microsoft.com/en-us/library/dd379511%28v=ws.10%29.aspx`.

Guest agents and driver installation on Windows guests

Like Linux guests, you can also install the guest agent and various drivers to get better performance and features for Windows workloads. All required guest agents and drivers for the Windows guest operating system will be available under the `rhev-tools-setup.iso` image by default. This is shipped on `rhev-guest-tools-iso.rpm` by default and gets installed on your RHEV-M system during the installation of the RHEV-M packages. It can be found at `/usr/share/rhev-guest-tools-iso/rhev-tools-setup.iso`.

Since we configured `/rhev-iso-library` on the RHEV-M system to act as a storage for the ISO domain, the `rhev-tools-setup.iso` file will be automatically copied to the ISO storage domain. If you are using any remote NFS server as the ISO storage domain, you need to upload these guest ISO files using the ISO uploader tool like we did to upload ISO images of the operating system installer in the previous chapter.

To install the guest agent and various drivers, have a look at the following steps:

1. Select the Windows virtual machine under the **Virtual Machines** tab, right-click on it, and select **Change CD**. Now, select **RHEV-toolsSetup_3.3_10.iso** from the drop-down menu, as shown in the following screenshot. This will attach the ISO file as a CD-ROM device to the windows guest.

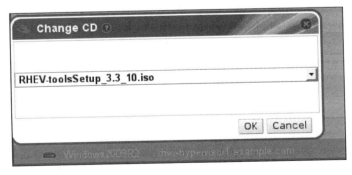

2. Right-click on the selected virtual machine again, and click on **Console** and log in to your Windows guest using the administrator credentials. Navigate to **Start | Computer**, select **CD-ROM drives** under the **Devices with Removable Storage** section of your Windows guest, and press *Enter*. This will expand the content of the ISO files.

3. Install the RHEV **Application Provisioning Tool (APT)**, which is a Windows service that can be installed in Windows virtual machines. Once it's installed, it will automatically scan the attached guest ISO files for valid guest tools' ISO and check your Windows guests against it. If there are no guest tools installed on the system already, it will automatically install all the required guest agents and drivers and reboot your Windows guest.

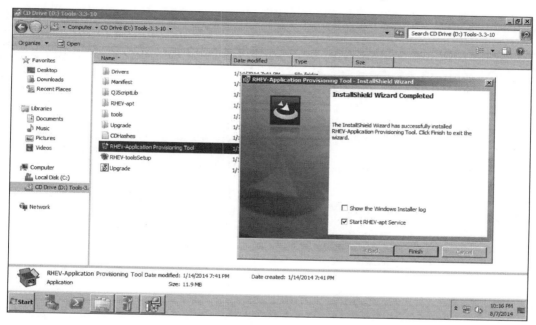

4. To check the list of guest agents and drivers installed on your Windows guest, navigate to the **Virtual Machines** tab, select the Windows guest, and click on **Applications** in the bottom pane.

If `RHEV-toolsSetup.iso` is updated in the future, the APT service will automatically attach the updated ISO file on the virtual machines where the APT service is enabled and running.

For more information on guest tools and its various drivers, please refer to the *RHEV Administration Guide Guest Drivers and Agents* section (section 17.8) in the RHEV Administration Guide available at `https://access.redhat.com/documentation/en-US/Red_Hat_Enterprise_Virtualization/3.3/html/Administration_Guide/sect-Guest_Drivers_and_Agents.html`.

Virtual machine templates

Now that you know how to create a virtual machine, you can save its settings to a template. This template will retain the original virtual machine's configurations, including virtual disk and network interface settings, operating systems, and applications. You can use this template to rapidly create replicas of the original virtual machine.

Creating a Red Hat Enterprise Linux template

To create a RHEL virtual machine template, you need to seal a virtual machine in order to remove a few important system-related settings so that they do not get propagated across the templates and on to the virtual machines that we are going to create using these templates. To seal a Linux virtual machine, follow these steps:

1. Log in to the virtual machine as a root, and perform the following configuration:

    `# touch /.unconfigured`

2. Remove SSH host keys:

    `# rm -rf /etc/ssh/ssh_host_*`

3. Modify the HOSTNAME parameter setting under the `/etc/sysconfig/network` file to `localhost.localdomain`.

4. Remove HWADDR= line from `/etc/sysconfig/network-scripts/ifcfg-eth*`.

5. Remove the network-related udev rule using the following command:

    `# rm -rf /etc/udev/rules.d/70-*`

6. Optionally, you can install any software packages that need to be common for all your Linux virtual machines, for example, RHEV guest agent's RPM. You can also remove any system logs that you don't want to propagate across the virtual machines created using these templates for any security reasons.

7. Finally, turn off the power of the virtual machine using the following command:

```
# poweroff
```

Alternatively, you can use cloud-init instead of following all the preceding steps. The Cloud-Init tool allows you to automate early configuration tasks in your virtual machines, including setting hostnames, authorized keys, and more. For detailed information on how to use cloud-init, please refer to the *Sealing Templates in Preparation for Deployment* section in RHEV 3.3 Administration Guide at `https://access.redhat.com/documentation/en-US/Red_Hat_Enterprise_Virtualization/3.3/html-single/Administration_Guide/index.html#sect-Using_Cloud-Init_to_Automate_the_Configuration_of_Virtual_Machines`.

Now, you are going to create a template out of this virtual machine using the following steps:

1. In the administration portal, click on the **Virtual Machines** tab. Select the sealed Red Hat Enterprise Linux 6 virtual machine.

2. Click on **Make Template**; this opens up the **New Template** creation window.

3. Enter the relevant information in the fields, such as the name of the template with a meaningful description and comment, host cluster, and optionally, the storage domains on which the template will be created by choosing the drop-down menu of the **Target** field.

4. If you enable **Allow all users to access this Template**, this template will be available to all the users. If you uncheck it, this template will only be available to the template creator and the admin user unless you provide permission to any specific user. We will study this in detail when assigning the user and group permissions in the upcoming chapter.

5. Finally, click on **OK**; this will change the status of your virtual machine to **Image Locked** until the time of the template creation. Once the template is created, the virtual machine status will change to **Down**, and you can see your new template ready for use and listed under the **Templates** tab of your admin portal. The **New Template** window along with all its properties is shown in the following screenshot:

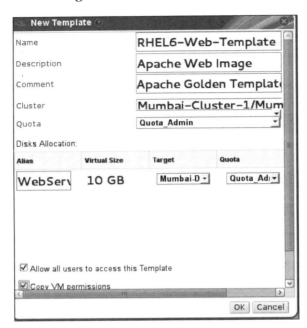

Cloning a RHEL virtual machine from a template

We created our first RHEL template with preinstalled operating system and configuration settings and along with preconfigured compute resources, such as network, storage, CPU, and memory. Now, you can use this template to clone a new RHEL virtual machine in a matter of seconds.

To clone a RHEL virtual machine from a template, have a look at the following steps:

1. Navigate to the **Virtual Machines** tab and click on **New Server**.

2. Under the **General** tab of the virtual machine creation windows, select the newly created template from the drop-down menu under **Based on Template**.

3. Enter a name with an appropriate description for your new virtual machine. The rest of the values will be inherited from the template, and optionally, you can also change them.

4. You can also change the storage allocation policy of your new virtual machine by clicking on **Show Advanced Options**. Move to the **Resource Allocation** tab and you will see that the **Storage Allocation** field will get enabled to choose the type of provisioning and storage allocation policy. If you set **Provisioning** as **Thin**, the virtual machine will depend upon the template it's created from, and it won't allow you to remove the template unless and until all the virtual machines created from the template are removed from the cluster.

   A clone does not depend on the template it was created from after it has been created. So, it's recommended that you choose **Clone** as the option for more flexibility, **Storage Allocation Policy** to **Preallocated** for the server and high I/O intensive workloads, and **Provisioning** as **Thin** for desktop workloads.

5. Retain all other default settings and click on **OK** to create the virtual machine. Cloning a virtual machine might take some time, and during this time the new virtual machine will have an **Image Locked** status before moving to the **Down** state. Finally, the virtual machine gets displayed in the virtual machines' list, and you can power on to set up the basic network setting to host your application.

Creating a Windows template

Similar to Linux guests, you can create a template for your Windows virtual machine in RHEV. Before creating a template based on an existing Windows virtual machine, remember that it has to be sealed with a Sysprep tool. This ensures that machine-related settings are not propagated through the template.

The procedure explained in this section is applicable for Windows 2008 R2 guests. If you wish to seal other versions of Windows, please refer to the following Windows documentation link on how to get and use Sysprep and seal the Windows guest before creating a template at `http://technet.microsoft.com/en-us/library/cc721940%28v=ws.10%29.aspx`.

You can use the `sysprep/generalize` command to reset Windows Product Activation a maximum of three times. If you plan to create more than three virtual machine templates with different preinstalled applications from a master Windows guest, a snapshot is required before sealing a Windows virtual machine every time. Once the template is created from the sealed master virtual machine, you can revert to the original snapshot of your master virtual machine before sealing the process and then update the master virtual machine and reseal it before creating a new template. For more information on virtual machine snapshots, please refer to the *Virtual machine snapshots* section in this chapter.

To seal a Windows virtual machine using Sysprep, perform the following steps:

1. Log in in as an admin user of the Windows virtual guest using the remote desktop utility or using the SPICE console.

2. Open a command-line terminal and type `regedit`. Now, in the **Registry Editor** window, navigate to **HKEY_LOCAL_MACHINE | SYSTEM | SETUP** from the left pane.

3. In the main window, navigate to **New | String value**. Insert `UnattendFile` as the value's name and press *Enter*. Right-click on the file and select **Modify**. In the **Edit String** dialog box, enter the value data as `a:\sysprep.ini`.

4. Now, launch the Sysprep tool by running `C:\Windows\System32\sysprep\sysprep.exe`. On the system preparation dialog box, please select the following:

   ◦ **System Cleanup Action**, select **Enter System Out-of-Box-Experience (OOBE)**

   ◦ Click on the **Generalize** checkbox to change the system identification number

   ◦ Under **Shutdown options**, select **Shutdown**

5. Finally, click on **OK**. Now, the virtual machine will go through sealing the process and will shut down automatically. Now, the Windows 2008 guest is sealed and ready to create a template in order to deploy virtual machines from the new template that we are going to create.

6. In the administration portal, click on the **Virtual Machines** tab. Select the sealed Windows 2008 virtual machine.

7. Click on **Make Template**. The **New Virtual Machine Template** window is displayed. Fill in all the required fields and click on **OK**. This will automatically create a new Windows 2008 template that we can use to deploy new virtual machines based on this template.

8. The rest of the steps that are required to create a virtual machine from the Windows template are the same as the ones we performed for the RHEL guest. Please follow the same procedure to create the Windows guest from the template.

Please refer to the *Create a Windows Template* section of RHEV 3.3 Evaluation Guide for more detailed information on modifying virtual machine template properties such as the time zone, enabling the template that joins Windows active directory services, and more at `https://access.redhat.com/documentation/en-US/Red_Hat_Enterprise_Virtualization/3.3/html/Evaluation_Guide/Windows_template_creation.html`.

Virtual machine snapshots

A snapshot is a state of your virtual machine at a particular point in time. This will be useful in order to preserve the state of your virtual machine before making any major changes to your operating system or application upgrades on a virtual machine. Creating a snapshot will allow you to restore the old state in the case of unintended sequences post your changes. RHEV supports live snapshots of your virtual machine.

Creating snapshots

The steps that create snapshots are common for any guest and are independent of the operating system running inside.

To create a snapshot, use the following steps: .

1. Navigate to the **Virtual Machines** tab, and select a virtual machine to take a snapshot. Right-click on it and select **Create Snapshot**. Give a meaningful name to the snapshot so that it will be easy to restore the proper snapshot in the future, leave the **Save Memory** option checked, and click on **OK**.

2. During the course of the snapshot creation, the virtual machine status changes from the up to the pause state and comes back to the up state post completion of the snapshot action.

3. To view the newly created snapshot, select the virtual machine and select snapshots from the bottom pane. This will give you a list of all the meaningful snapshots created for the virtual machine. Select the snapshot and explore the **General, Disks, Network Interfaces**, and **Installed Application** options on the right-hand side of the same window to view the details about the snapshot.

Restoring virtual machines from the snapshot

To restore virtual machines from the snapshot, select the virtual machine and click on **Snapshots** in the bottom pane, and perform the following steps. Before this, you need to power off the virtual machine in order to merge the snapshot:

1. Select the snapshot you intend to restore, and click on **Preview** to preview the snapshot. The status of the virtual machine briefly changes to **Image Locked** before returning to **Down**.

2. Now, start the virtual machine, which will start from the state of the disk image of the snapshot. The preview will give you the flexibility to cross-check the virtual machine state. If you feel that this is the state to which you want to restore your virtual machine, you can now shut down the virtual machine and go to the **Snapshots** tab in the bottom pane.

3. Click on **Commit** to restore the virtual machine to this state; this will erase all the subsequent snapshots taken after that.

4. If you want to undo and roll back to the last state, you can click on **Undo**. By clicking on **Commit** or **Undo**, the virtual machine will go to the **Image Locked** state briefly and will come back to the **Down** state. Now, you can power on the virtual machine.

 Note that **Preview** and **Commit** is recommended to cross-check the state of the virtual machine. If you are confident about the state of the virtual machine, you can directly click on **Preview** and then on **Commit** to restore the intended state.

Creating a virtual machine from the snapshot

RHEV also supports the creation of a virtual machine from the snapshots of the virtual machine. To create a virtual machine from the snapshots, use the following steps:

1. Select the virtual machine, and click on the **Snapshots** tab in the bottom pane. This will list all the available snapshots for this virtual machine.

2. Select the snapshot and click on **Clone**. This will open a new window that will clone the virtual machine from the snapshot.

3. Fill in the **Name** and **Description** fields and then click on **OK**. This will create a new virtual machine based on the snapshot.

Deleting a virtual machine snapshot

To delete a virtual machine snapshot, select the virtual machine and shut down if it is in the power-on state. Removing the snapshot does not affect the virtual machine. To delete a virtual machine snapshot, perform the following steps:

1. Click on the **Snapshots** tab in the bottom pane and then delete the selected snapshot by clicking on **Delete**. This will open up a deletion confirmation window; click on **OK** to delete the snapshot permanently.

2. To check the status of a **Create** or **Delete** operation, you can use the **Events** and **Tasks** buttons provided under the bottom pane of your admin portal. Select the respective button, and click on the up arrow sign to expand it.

3. Power on the virtual machine once the snapshot deletion is completed successfully.

Backing up virtual machines to export disks

In RHEV, you can back up your virtual machines and templates to an export disk. Why do we need this? This option will allow you to move virtual machines or templates from one data center to another in the same environment or to a completely new RHEV environment. This will also allow you to back up your virtual machine and template to restore it at later point of time. The virtual machine must be in the powered-off state before exporting the virtual machine to the export disk.

Alternatively, you can use the backup API for the live backup and restoration of your virtual machine. To learn more about the backup API, please refer to the RHEV 3.3 **Developer Guide** at `https://access.redhat.com/documentation/en-US/ Red_Hat_Enterprise_Virtualization/3.3/html/Developer_Guide/Backup- Restore_API_Overview.html`.

Exporting a virtual machine and template

To export a virtual machine, you must have an active export storage domain in your data center. If you remember, we configured and activated an export domain in *Chapter 3, Setting Up the RHEV Virtual Infrastructure*. We are going to use this domain to export a virtual machine and templates.

To export a virtual machine, use the following steps:

1. Select the virtual machine to export and shut down the virtual machine.
2. Right-click on the virtual machine, and click on **Export**. In the **Export Virtual Machine** window, you will find the following two options:
   - **Force Override**: This will override existing images of the virtual machine on the export domain.
   - **Collapse Snapshots**: This creates a single export volume per disk. It also removes the dependency of the template that is available on the data center where we are going to import the virtual machine later. It's applicable only if the exported virtual machine is created from the virtual machine template.
3. The procedure to export the virtual machine template is identical to the previous process. To export a template, navigate to the **Templates** tab, select the template, and right-click on it to select the **Export** option.

The virtual machine or template exportation is a time-consuming operation; check the **Events** and **Tasks** tab to track the status. Upon successful completion of the exportation, navigate to the **Storage** tab, select **Export Domain**, and click on the **VM Import** tab or the **Template Import** tab. You will see the exported virtual machine or template listed there.

Importing a virtual machine and template

In the previous section, we learned how to export a virtual machine and template. Once the virtual machine or template is exported, you can import these back to a new data center in the same RHEV environment or a new environment. The steps to import the virtual machine or template in both the scenarios are the same. However, we need to attach the export domain to a new data center.

To import a virtual machine or template within the same RHEV environment, perform the following steps:

1. Navigate to the **Storage** tab and select the export domain. Now, select the **Data Center** tab from the bottom pane.

2. Select the data center to which this export domain is attached and click on **Maintenance**. This will put the export domain in the maintenance state.

3. Once it goes to the maintenance state, select **Detach** on the same window. This will detach the export domain from the data center and the status of the export domain changes to **Unattached**.

4. Now, to attach to the other data center in the same RHEV environment, select **Unattached Export Domain** from the **Storage** tab.

5. Then, select the **Data Center** tab from the bottom pane, and click on **Attach**. A new window will open with a list of all the available active data centers in your environment. Select the data center where you want to attach this export domain to import the virtual machine or templates.

6. Once you click on **OK**, the status of the export domain will change from the **Maintenance** to **Locked** state for a few seconds, and then, it will switch to the **Active** state.

7. To import the virtual machine from the export disk, select the export domain and click on **VM Import** from the bottom pane. Select the virtual machine and click on **Import**.

8. In the new import virtual machine window, select the data storage domain and the cluster on which you want to import the virtual machine. Also, if you select **Collapse Snapshots** or **Clone** in the bottom pane of the same window, it will give you the option to convert your virtual machine storage allocation policy to either **Thin** or **Preallocated** under the **Disk** section. Click on **OK** to start the import process.

 Importation is a slow process, and depends upon the size of the virtual machine image and your performance of the storage and network. Keep an eye on the **Events** tab to track the status of completion.

To import the virtual machine or template to a different RHEV environment, perform the following steps:

1. Remove the export domain from the active RHEV environment.

2. Log in to the admin portal of your new RHEV environment. Navigate to the **Storage** tab. Make sure that the NFS export disk is accessible by the entire host in the data center of your new RHEV environment.

3. Click on **Import Domain** and select the **Data Center** and **Domain Function Storage** type from the drop-down menu.

4. Select the host from the **Use Host** drop-down menu to perform this initial operation.

5. Under **Export Path**, enter `nfsserverfqdn:/export-path`. This is `storage.example.com:/export/rhev_import_export_disk` in our case.

6. Click on **OK**, and the window will start loading with the **Importing new storage domain** message. After a few seconds, the newly imported and exported domains will be listed under the **Storage** tab with the status in the **Locked** state. Finally, the status will change from **Locked** to **Up**.

7. Select the export domain, and click on the **VM Import** tab or **Template Import** tab. This will list all your virtual machines and templates that are exported and ready to be imported to your new RHEV environment.

8. Follow the same step that we followed to import the virtual machine or template on a different data center in the same RHEV environment to import virtual machines and templates on your new RHEV environment.

 Only one export domain will be attached and remain active in a data center at a point in time.

Summary

In this chapter, we discussed in detail how to create Linux and Windows virtual machines and their templates and guest agent's installations in order to enhance performance. We also learned how to create a virtual machine from templates, clone a new virtual machine from templates, and learned about the virtual machine snapshot features of RHEV, such as creating and restoring virtual machines from snapshots. Finally, we learned how to export the virtual machines and templates so that they can be imported to other data centers in the same RHEV environment as well as how to import them to a newer RHEV environment.

In the next chapter, we will discuss high availability features of RHEV, including how to enable high availability for virtual machines and set different priorities, host high availability and cluster policies, and live migration of virtual machines across the hosts in a cluster, and more.

5
Virtual Machine and Host High Availability

So far, we have learned how to set up a basic Red Hat Enterprise Virtualization infrastructure, and spinned up Linux and Windows virtual instances with advanced topics such as virtual machine snapshots, templates, and more. In this chapter, we will learn about a few more advanced high-availability functions of Red Hat Enterprise Virtualization, such as the following:

- Virtual machine's live migration
- Virtual machine's high availability
- Hosting high-availability and cluster policies

Virtual machine's live migration

Virtual machine's live migration allows you to move live running virtual machines from one physical server to another. In short, from one RHEV hypervisor host to another, it is also possible to migrate non-live virtual machines from one host to another in RHEV. During the course of live migration, the virtual machine remains powered on, and the application hosted on it continues to serve the end user without any loss in network connectivity or application access while relocating from one host to another.

Migration works by sending the state of the virtual machine memory and all its virtualized devices to a destination host. In live migration, virtual machine memory pages are transferred to the destination host. RHEV monitors the guest memory page transfer from the source to the destination host and also estimates the transfer speed. If the estimated period of migration goes beyond the default configurable time of 10 minutes, RHEV suspends the original guest machine on the source host, transfers the remaining data, and resumes the same guest on the destination host.

In offline or cold migration, RHEV suspends the guest virtual machine before moving the image of the virtual machine memory to the destination host. After a successful transfer of the memory pages, the virtual machine is resumed back on the destination host.

Each live migration event is limited to a maximum transfer speed of 30 MBps, and the number of concurrent migrations supported is also limited by default, and it's tunable in the hypervisor vdsm configuration file. The time it takes to complete such a migration depends on the network bandwidth and latency. If the network is experiencing heavy use or low bandwidth, the migration will take much longer.

Advantages of live migration

There are primarily three main advantages of live migration:

- **Load balancing**: RHEV lets you move the virtual machine running on the overloaded host to an underutilized host in order to ensure smoother functioning of business-critical workloads without any service interruption

- **Hardware or software maintenance**: If there is a need to upgrade, add, or remove any hardware, and in the case of a planned software upgrade, you can safely relocate the guest operating system, without any downtime, to other active hypervisor hosts at any time

- **Power saving**: By using live migration, one can consolidate the guest operating system to switch on to the set of hosts in the cluster and power off the remaining set of hosts in order to save energy and cut down power costs during low usage and non-business hours

The requirements of live migration

For live or cold migration to work in RHEV, the following are the minimum prerequisites that should be met:

- The source and destination host must be a part of the same cluster in RHEV

- Hosts must be in up status and must access the same virtual networks and VLANs

- Enough compute resources, such as CPU capacity and RAM, must be available on the destination host

- Both the source and destination hosts must have access to the data storage domain on which the virtual machine images reside

- Shared storage, such as network storage or fiber channel SAN to store the virtual machine images
- It is strongly recommended that you dedicate a logical network for the live migration traffic by splitting management, virtual machine data, and storage traffic using a dedicated logical network to minimize the risk of network saturation

Manual live migration

In order to manually perform live migration on a running virtual machine from one host to another in RHEV, perform the following steps:

1. Log in to the **Administrator** portal and navigate to the **Virtual Machine** tab.
2. Select the virtual machine you want to migrate and right-click on it.
3. Select **Migrate**; this will open a new pop-up window with two options, as shown in the following screenshot:

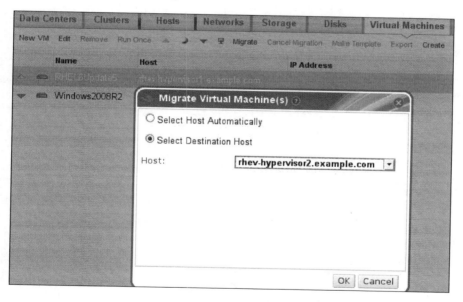

4. If the **Select Host Automatically** option is selected, then RHEV determines the host to which the virtual machine is to be migrated according to the load-balancing or power-saving policy defined in the cluster. We will learn more about cluster policy, in detail, later on in this chapter.
5. The **Select Destination Host** option will allow you to select the host from the drop-down menu as the destination host for the virtual machine.

6. Select the appropriate option relevant to your environment, and click on **OK**.

7. For a couple of seconds, you will see that the status of the virtual machine changes from **Up** to **Migrating From**, and finally, the status changes back to **Up** after a successful migration.

Now, you can see the virtual machine that runs on the different destination hosts based on the selection, and this can be seen under the **Host** column of the virtual machine we migrated.

Cold migration

Cold migration or offline migration is nothing but migrating the powered-off virtual machine from one host to another. Follow the same steps as the ones outlined in the preceding *Manual live migration* section to migrate the powered-off virtual machine to a new destination in the same cluster.

Cancelling migration

If the virtual machine migration is taking longer than expected, then you can cancel the live migration by selecting the virtual machine that is in the **Migrating** status and right-clicking on **Cancel Migration**.

Virtual machine's high availability

Virtual machine's high availability is one of the key aspects that need to be considered when someone is hosting their business-critical application on virtualization. High availability means that a virtual machine will be automatically restarted if it is terminated for a reason other than intentional shutdown by the administrator from the guest operating system console or RHEV Manager admin console. A high availability virtual machine is automatically restarted either on its original host or another host in the cluster.

This is achieved due to the way the RHEV Manager is intelligently designed to constantly monitor the health of the hosts, storage, hardware failure, and more to restart the failed, highly available virtual machine without any manual intervention and with minimal interruption to the service.

Generally, high availability will kick in on the following scenarios:

- When the hardware of the host fails
- When the host loses its connectivity with the storage or network
- When a watchdog card is attached and enabled in virtual machines

An RHEV cluster consists of a group of hosts that you can configure for high availability. In a cluster, you can configure the cluster policy to be in either the load-balancing or power-saving mode. Under either mode, one of the cluster policies is enabled; the virtual machine will be automatically live migrated based on the overall load of the cluster. You can also restrict the automatic migration of the virtual machine, keeping the cluster policy enabled by pinning the virtual machine to a specific host, thereby allowing manual migration that suits some specific application use cases.

Before enabling the high availability of virtual machines, the host should be configured for high availability. A highly available host requires a power-management device and its fencing parameters configured. High availability will only work if the fencing succeeds. For more information on power management, please refer to the *High-availability hosting* and *Cluster policies* sections later in this chapter.

To configure a highly available virtual machine, perform the following steps:

1. Log in to the **Administrator** portal, and navigate to the **Virtual Machine** tab.
2. Select the appropriate virtual machine, right-click on it, and select **Edit**.
3. In the **Edit Virtual Machine** window, select **Show Advanced Options**, and move to the **High Availability** tab.
4. Check the **Highly Available** radio button and set the **Priority for Run/Migration queue** option as **Low**, **Medium**, or **High**—whichever is feasible for you.
5. Click on **OK** to save and close it.

Automatic virtual machine migration

Red Hat Enterprise Virtualization will automatically initiate the live migration of all the running virtual machines that are marked as highly available and not pinned on a specific host when the host is moved to the maintenance mode. This will be specifically helpful in a scenario such as the major hardware fault of the hosts running hundreds of virtual machines during critical business hours so that the admin does not need to manually select all the hundred virtual machines and migrate them manually.

During the course of automatic virtual machine migration, the destination host in which these virtual machines are to be placed will be selected based on the cluster policy defined for the cluster. By default, the cluster policy is selected as none and it's strongly recommended that you select the cluster policy of either load balancing or power saving, whichever suits your environment.

When a virtual server is automatically migrated because of the high-availability function, the details of the automatic migration are documented in the **Events** tab of the RHEV Manager console.

In the case of hardware failure of one of the hypervisors in a cluster that runs two hypervisor hosts, only virtual machines marked as highly available will be restarted, provided that there are enough compute resources available on the second host. The rest of the virtual machines will be in the power-down state even though they're marked highly available due to resource constraints.

The migration priority

Red Hat Enterprise Virtualization supports concurrent migration requests by queuing the migration request of virtual machines, and it will also allow you to define the migration priority of virtual machines based on the application SLA and business criticality.

By setting the migration priority based upon workloads, the virtual machine with high priority will be migrated first, followed by medium and low.

Perform the following steps to set the migration priority for a virtual machine:

1. Log in to the **Administrator** portal, and navigate to the **Virtual Machine** tab.
2. Select the appropriate virtual machine, right-click on it, and select **Edit**.
3. In the **Edit Virtual Machine** window, select **Show Advanced Options**, and move to the **High Availability** tab.

4. Check the **Highly Available** radio button, and set the **Priority for Run/Migration queue** option as **Low**, **Medium**, or **High** — whichever is feasible for you.

5. Click on **OK** to save and close it.

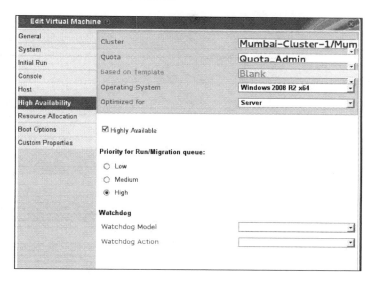

Disabling the automatic virtual machine migration

There are a few use cases, such as using Red Hat's high-availability add-on inside the Red Hat Enterprise Linux guest operating system for the application's high availability or Cluster Suite on the RHEV infrastructure, where we need to disable the automatic virtual machine migration. This can be achieved by pinning the virtual machine to run only on a specific host. Pinning the virtual machine to run only on the selected host will prevent the automatic live migration in the case of that specific host's failure.

To pin a virtual machine to a specific host, perform the following steps.

1. Log in to the **Administrator** portal, and navigate to the **Virtual Machine** tab.

2. Select the appropriate virtual machine, right-click on it, and select **Edit**.

3. In the **Edit Virtual Machine** window, select **Show Advanced Options**, as shown in the following screenshot.

4. Move to the **Host** tab, select **Start Running On**, uncheck **Any host the Cluster**, select the **Specific** radio button, and select the host from the drop-down menu.

5. Finally, under the **Migration Options** drop-down menu, select **Do not allow migration**, and click on **OK**.

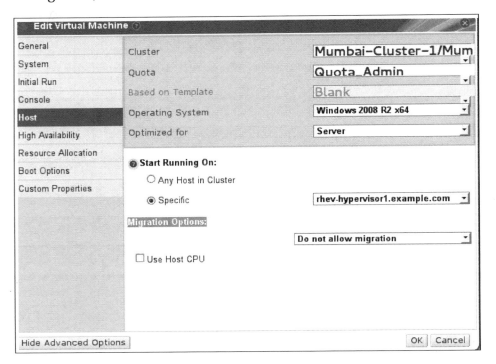

The host's high availability

The Red Hat Enterprise Virtualization manager constantly monitors the status and health of hypervisor hosts using heartbeat messages over the management network called **RHEV-M**. There are two main error states that the hypervisor host will turn on.

If the host state changes to **Non Responsive**, it clearly indicates that the hypervisor lost communication with the manager. Under such a scenario, the RHEV Manager tries to recover the nonresponsive host by initiating the fence operation using power management options. For fencing to work, you need at least one active host in the cluster or in the data center.

The RHEV Manager does not directly connect to the fencing device to perform power-management operations. Instead, the RHEV Manager chooses one of the active hypervisors in the cluster as a proxy in order to perform the fence command.

After the successful fence operation, all the virtual machines that are marked as highly available and were earlier running on the troubled host will get restarted in other active hosts in the same cluster.

Once the fenced host turns to the **Up** state after the reboot operation, the cluster policy kicks in to load balance the virtual workloads on a newly rebooted host. This is where the RHEV cluster policy will be greatly helpful for you to load balance your virtual workloads. If the fenced host does not come up in the prescribed time, then the host status changes to **Non Responsive**, and it needs manual intervention for further troubleshooting.

Sometimes, the host state changes to **Non Operational**; this is mainly due to the incorrect configuration of hosts, such as missing logical networks for that host or due to the inability to access the storage domains or LUNs.

To troubleshoot such scenarios, please refer to the **Events** tab on the bottom pane of the **Manager Administrator** console for detailed logs.

Manual fencing

If the hypervisor host without the power management configured in a cluster or data center went to the **Non Responsive** state due to some hardware failure, it will significantly affect the overall performance of your virtual infrastructure, thereby causing all the virtual machines running on the host to change to the **Unknown** status. In such cases, we need to manually fence or isolate the nonresponsive host by manually rebooting the host or powering it down to recover all the virtual machines. Once the host is rebooted or powered down manually, perform the following steps:

1. Log in to the **Administrator** console, and navigate to the **Host** tab.

2. Select the **Non responsive** host, right-click on it, and select the **Confirm Host has been rebooted** button.

3. A warning window will pop up to ensure that the host has been shut down or rebooted; select **Approve Operation**, and click on **OK**.

4. Post this, all the virtual machines marked highly available that were running on the failed host will turn to the power-down state and allow us to get restarted on other active hosts in the cluster.

> Do not use the **Confirm host has been rebooted** option unless you have manually rebooted the host. Using this option while the host is still running can lead to a virtual machine image corruption. For more information on the power management configuration, please refer to Red Hat Enterprise Virtualization Admin Guide.

Cluster policies

The Red Hat Enterprise Virtualization cluster resilience policy allows you to define the migration policy for virtual machines in the event of host failure. There might be a possibility of a physical host failure in such conditions. The migration of the running virtual machine decision to be automatic or manual purely depends upon the cluster resilience policy defined by the admin.

There are situations where a physical host runs more than a dozen virtual machines. Since the virtual machine migration is a network-intensive operation, it's highly recommended that you choose the best policy that suits your environment. Under this kind of scenario, the best approach is to choose **Migrate only highly-available virtual machine** as the policy to avoid unnecessary network saturation by moving dozens of virtual machines.

The resilience policy

There are three cluster resilience policies that you can define in RHEV. To define cluster the resilience policy, perform the following steps:

1. Log in to the **Administrator** console, and navigate to the **Clusters** tab.

2. Select the appropriate cluster from the list for which you want to define the resilience policy, right-click on it, and select **Edit**.

3. In the new **Edit Cluster** window, move to **Resilience Policy**, and select any of the following options relevant to your environment:

   ◦ **Migrate Virtual Machines**: This will migrate all the virtual machines in the order of their defined priority

   ◦ **Migrate only Highly Available Virtual Machines**: This will migrate only highly available virtual machines in order to prevent overloading on other hosts

   ◦ **Do Not Migrate Virtual Machines**: This will prevent virtual machines from being migrated

The cluster policy

The cluster policy will allow you to distribute the load of virtual machine across hosts in the cluster. By default, **Cluster Policy** is set to **None**.

Perform the following steps to define a new cluster policy:

1. Log in to the **Administrator** console, and navigate to the **Clusters** tab.

2. Select the appropriate cluster from the list for which you want to define the cluster policy, right-click on it, and select **Edit**.

3. In the new **Edit Cluster** window, move to **Cluster Policy**, and select any of the following options relevant to your environment:

    ○ **Evenly_Distributed**: Distribute the CPU load evenly across the hosts in the cluster. If any of the hosts in the cluster breach the defined maximum service level, the additional virtual machine will not start on the specific host.

    ○ **CpuOverCommitDurationMinutes**: This option allows you to define the time interval before the cluster policy takes an action. This is mainly to protect the unnecessary virtual machine migration due to a temporary spike in the CPU load.

    ○ **HighUtilization**: This is defined in percentage. If the host CPU reaches this defined limit or crosses it, then the RHEV Manager will start to migrate the virtual machine to another underutilized host until the defined CPU limit of the host falls under an accepted threshold.

    ○ **Power saving**: Setting the policy will distribute the CPU load across subsets of other hosts. In short, if any hosts in the cluster fall under the low CPU utilization limit for the defined time interval, then the RHEV Manager will start to migrate the running virtual machine to another underutilized host and allow us to safely power down the hosts that are not running any virtual machines. This is extremely useful during non-business hours where systems are running with less load in order to save power. Note that if the other active host CPU limit reaches the high utilization CPU limit, then the additional virtual machine will not start on the host.

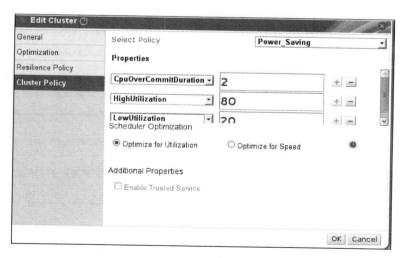

Summary

In this chapter, we discussed the various high-availability features of hosts and virtual machines available in Red Hat Enterprise Virtualization in detail. This includes the live and cold migration of virtual machines, automatic migration and setting up migration priority for virtual machines, host resilience policy, and finally, defining various cluster policies, such as even distribution and power saving, to distribute virtual workloads for better performance and to save power.

In the next chapter, we will discuss advanced storage options such as using sharing disks for high-availability cluster applications inside guest operating systems running on RHEV, attaching direct storage LUN mapping to a virtual machine for I/O-intensive database workloads, moving virtual machines across different storage domains, and finally, shaping network traffic using the VNIC profile for guest operating systems and hot plugs of network adapter and memory to virtual machines.

6
Advanced Storage and Networking Features

In the previous chapter, we learned various high-availability features supported by Red Hat Enterprise Virtualization. Now, it's time to move on and learn some advanced storage features offered in Red Hat Enterprise Virtualization, such as sharing disks across multiple virtual machines for an application's high availability using cluster software that needs shared storage access and raw device mapping of direct LUN from storage for workloads that are I/O intensive such as database, resize guest virtual disks, and moving live virtual machine disks across storage domains in the data center.

Set up a **Virtual Network Interface Card (VNIC)** profile to apply network **Quality of Service (QoS)** that allows you to control the network's resource usage based on the user level, hot plug of virtual disks, and the virtual network adapter to the guest operating system that runs on Red Hat Enterprise Virtualization.

In this chapter, we will cover the following topics:

- Shareable disks
- Direct **Logical Unit Number (LUN)** mapping
- Virtual disk resize
- Storage live migration
- VNIC QoS
- Hot plugging devices

Shareable disks

The floating disk or shareable disks feature of Red Hat Enterprise Virtualization will allow you to carve out a new virtual disk with the shareable option enabled. Virtual disks marked shareable are independent of any virtual machines and can be attached to a single or multiple numbers of virtual machines. This will be useful in scenarios where an application requires storage to be shared across virtual machines and integrated with high-availability cluster software on those virtual machines to create a group of cluster nodes with shared storage access.

Please be careful while using floating disks. Using shareable disks and mounting the shared disks across multiple virtual machines at the same time (without using any cluster-aware software to coordinate disk read and write of the mounted file system) leads to data corruption. For example, you can use floating disks across two virtual machines and build an active/passive cluster service using Red Hat's high-availability add-on, or you can share it across three virtual machines and integrate it with the cluster filesystem, such as Red Hat **Global File System 2 (GF2)** for simultaneous read/write across all three nodes using the floating disk as a shared storage.

You can create a new sharing disk, or mark any of the existing disks as a sharing disk and attach it to the virtual machine. To create a new sharing disk, perform the following steps:

1. Log in to the **Administrator** console and navigate to the **Disks** tab.

2. Click on **Add** to open the **Add Virtual Disk** window, and you will see that by default, **Internal** is selected on the upper-left side of the window; leave it as it is.

3. Insert the disk size in the **Size (GB)** field, and then insert some meaningful content in the **Alias** and **Description** fields. Leave the **Interface** field as **Virtio** and **Allocation policy** as **Preallocated**. Select **Data Center** from the drop-down menu, select the respective storage domain from the drop-down menu, and leave the **Quota** field as the default value **Quota_Admin**.

4. On the top-right hand corner of the same window, select the **Is Shareable** and **Wipe After Delete** options. Finally, click on **OK** to create the virtual disk and close the window.

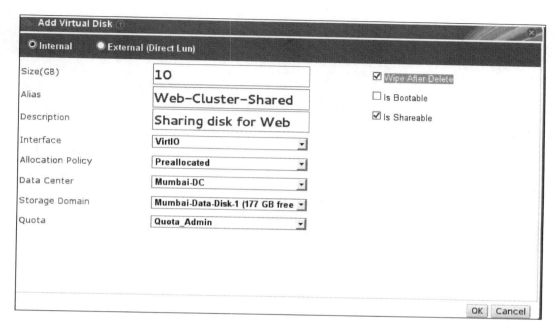

Now, the newly created sharing virtual disk will be listed under the **Disks** tab with the **OK** status and the **Attached to** column list null.

After you create the new virtual disk that is to be shared between virtual machines, it's now time to turn to attach that disk to two or more virtual machines. To do so, please follow these steps:

1. Log in to the **Administrator** console and navigate to the **Virtual machines** tab.

2. Select the appropriate virtual machine and navigate to **Disks** at the bottom pane of the selected virtual machine.

3. Click on **Add**; this will open up an **Add Virtual Disk** window. Select the **Attach Disk** radio button at the upper-left corner of the window. Select the sharing disk we created in the earlier step from the list. Leave the **Activate** button check marked, and click on **OK** to attach the sharing disk to the selected virtual machine and close the window.

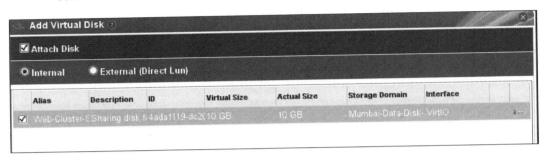

This will attach and activate the newly created sharing disk to the selected virtual machine, and the same thing can be cross-checked from the virtual machine's **Disks** tab at the bottom pane as well as in the event log of the manager console. To verify newly added shared disk from the guest operating system running Linux, please use the standard tool such as fdisk from the command line.

Repeat the same step to attach the same sharing virtual disk to two or more virtual machines.

Direct LUN mapping

Like sharing disk, users can also attach direct LUNs to virtual machines in Red Hat Enterprise Virtualization, which allow for the same sharing as a normal disk image. The LUN from the SAN is connected to the hypervisor hosting the virtual machines via a host bus adapter of the host through which all the storage I/O takes place. A LUN is a number used to identify a logical unit related to computer storage. A logical unit is a device addressed by protocols and related to fiber channel, **Small Computer System Interface (SCSI)**, **Internet SCSI (iSCSI)**, and other comparable interfaces.

There are a few considerations that the end user has to keep in mind before using the direct LUN on virtual machines:

- Direct LUN from the storage must be presented to all the hosts in the data center for the live migration of the virtual machine attached with direct LUN to work.

- Exporting virtual machine direct LUN disk to RHEV export domain is not supported. Export of such virtual machines only exports other disks except the direct LUN.

- Live storage migration of virtual machine direct LUN is not supported, while other disks of such virtual machine can be moved across storage domains.

- Direct LUN will not be a part of virtual machine snapshots.

So, to attach a direct LUN from the storage to virtual machine, please follow these steps:

1. Log in to the **Administrator** console and navigate to the **Disks** tab.

2. Click on **Add** to open the **Add Virtual Disk** window and select **External (Direct Lun)** on the upper-right side of the window.

3. Insert some meaningful content in the **Alias** and **Description** fields; leave the **Interface** field as **Virtio**, select **Data Center** from the drop-down menu, choose the host from the **Use Host** drop-down menu, and set the storage type to either **iSCSI** or **Fibre Channel** based on what is relevant to your environment.

   This will result in immediate scanning of all the LUNs visible to the selected host and display the list of available LUNs to use from the storage as mentioned in the following screenshot.

4. Select the LUN. You can optionally choose **Is Bootable** and **Is Shareable** if there is a need to present this direct LUN in the sharing mode to multiple virtual machines that run any high-availability cluster applications. Finally, click on **OK** to create a new direct LUN and close the window.

5. To check the newly created direct LUN, navigate to the **Disks** tab. This will display a list of all the disks by default, select the direct LUN, which will filter and list only the created and active direct LUNs that can be used to attach to the virtual machines.

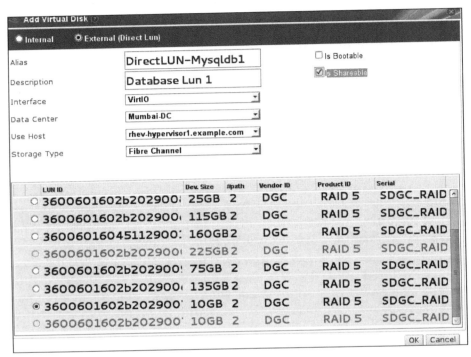

To attach the direct LUN to a virtual machine, perform the following steps:

1. Log in to the **Administrator** console and navigate to the **Virtual machines** tab.

2. Select the appropriate virtual machine and navigate to **Disks** at the bottom pane of the selected virtual machine.

3. Click on **Add**; this will open up an **Add Virtual Disk** window. Select the **Attach Disk** radio button at the top-left corner of the window. Select the **External (Direct Lun)** radio button, and select from the list of attached direct LUNs we created in the earlier step. Leave the **Activate** button check marked, and click on **OK** to attach the direct LUN attached to the selected virtual machine and close the window.

4. This will attach and activate the newly created direct LUN to the selected virtual machine, and the same thing can be cross-checked from the **Virtual Machine Disks** tab. Selecting the **All** radio button on the bottom pane as well as in the event log of the manager console. To verify from the guest operating system running Linux, please use the standard tools such as `fdisk` from the command line.

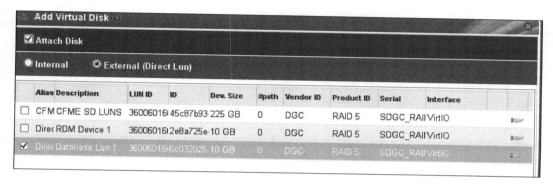

Since we selected the **Is Shareable** option while creating the direct LUN, users can attach the direct LUN to two or more virtual machines as per their need.

Virtual disk resize

In RHEV 3.3 and later, one can perform a resize of a virtual guest disk without taking the downtime of the virtual guest so that users don't have to change application or data locations that run on those virtual machines. To perform an online virtual disk resize of the running guest, perform these steps:

1. Log in to the **Administrator** console and navigate to the **Virtual machines** tab.

2. Select the appropriate virtual machine and navigate to **Disks** at the bottom pane of the selected virtual machine.

3. Select the disk and click on **Edit**. Under **Extend size by(GB)**, type the disk size in GB to be added to extend the existing virtual disk size (as shown in the following diagram). Note that the target disk status should be changed to **Locked** status during the time when it's being resized, and then changed to **OK** after its been resized.

4. Online virtual disk resize is not supported for floating or shareable disks, and shrinking the virtual disk is also not supported.

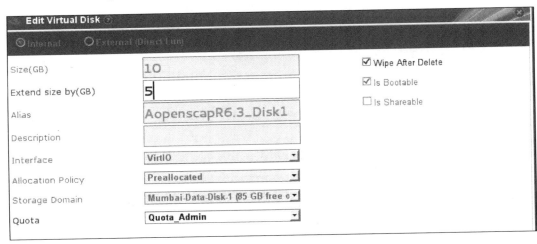

Alternatively, if application or data locations of virtual machines is not on priority, one can resize the disk size of the Linux guest with LVM as a root storage (by adding another disk), and extend the logical volume. Similarly, for Windows guests, disk resize can be achieved using the built-in disk management tool using dynamic disks supported in the latest version of the Windows operating system as an alternative to the preceding steps in extending the virtual disk.

Storage live migration

RHEV storage live migration of virtual hard disks allows you to move the virtual machine hard disks from one storage domain to another storage domain in the same data center without powering off the virtual machine. This will be useful in a scenario when the current storage domain where the virtual machine hard disk resides is running out of space, to move the virtual machine workloads to high- or low-performance storage based on demand, or to migrate from one type of storage to another type of storage prior to the decommission of one of your storage domains.

To move a virtual machine hard disk from one storage data domain to another domain, follow these steps:

1. Log in to the **Administrator** console and navigate to the **Virtual machines** resource tab.

2. Select the appropriate virtual machine and navigate to the **Disks** subtab on the bottom pane.

3. Select the virtual disk/disks and then right-click on it/them. Then, click on the **Move** option.

4. On the **Move Disk** window, select the **Target Storage** domain from the drop-down menu.

5. Click on **OK** to move, and close the window.

During the course of migration, the disk status changes to **Locked** while being moved, and the status changes back to **Up** when the virtual hard disk has moved to the target domain.

VNIC QoS

A VNIC profile allows users to create different VNIC profiles with a collection of different settings, such as network QoS, enable or disable port mirroring, and more, and apply these profiles to the individual virtual interface card attached to the virtual machines. This feature will enable the administrator to define a different profile with a custom limit in the inbound and outbound network traffic based on users or a service level while building a cloud using Red Hat Enterprise Virtualization.

Network QoS will allow the user to limit the inbound and outbound network traffic in the virtual NIC level. This kind of traffic shaping allows the network administrator to prevent overconsumption of network resources by limiting the bandwidth of both inbound and outbound traffic at the virtual NIC level.

So, as a first step, we need to define a new QoS profile at the RHEV data center level. To define a QoS, perform these steps:

1. Log in to the **Administrator** console and navigate to the **Data Center** resource tab.

2. Choose the appropriate data center and select the **Network QoS** tab from the bottom pane; click on **New** to create a new network QoS.

3. Enter a name for the new network QoS and define the QoS properties to limit the inbound and outbound traffic of the profile.

QoS currently includes the following properties:

- Inbound
    - **Average**: This is the long-term limit around which traffic should float (Mbps)
    - **Peak**: This is the maximum bandwidth allowed during burst (Mbps)
    - **Burst**: This is the burst size (MB)

- Outbound
    - **Average**: This is the long-term limit around which traffic should float (Mbps)
    - **Peak**: This is the maximum bandwidth allowed during burst (Mbps)
    - **Burst**: This is the burst size (MB)

From the settings shown in the following screenshot, after sending 50 MB with a data rate of 200 Mbps, the rate will drop to 100 Mbps:

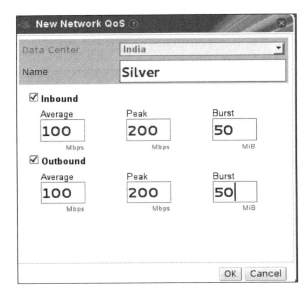

Now we can use the created QoS profile and attach it to a VNIC, also known as a **Virtual Machine (VM)** interface profile. Starting with Red Hat Enterprise Virtualization 3.3, when you create a new logical network from the manager, a VNIC profile of the same name as the logical network is automatically created under that logical network. We can also create multiple VNIC profiles, and apply those profiles to respective virtual machines.

To create a new VNIC profile, perform these steps:

1. Log in to the **Administrator** console and navigate to the **Networks** resource tab.

2. Select the appropriate logical network and click on the **Profiles** tab in the bottom pane.

3. Click on **New** and this will open a new **VM Interface Profile** window.

4. Insert some meaningful content in the **Name** and **Description** fields, and select the QoS profile you created from the drop-down menu.

5. Optionally, one can enable the **Port Mirroring** option; this will copy layer 3 network traffic on a given logical network and host to a virtual interface on a virtual machine, which can be used for network tuning, debugging, and more.

6. Finally, enable or disable **Allow all users to use this Profile**, and click on **OK** to save this profile and close the window.

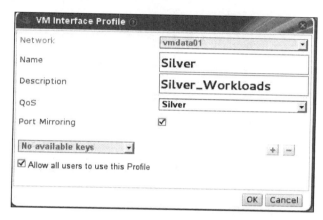

Now, we have created a VNIC profile with QoS defined, and to attach this QoS to the specific virtual machine virtual network interface, follow these steps:

1. Log in to the **Administrator** console, navigate to the **Virtual machines** resource tab, and select the appropriate virtual machine.

2. Navigate to the **Network Interfaces** tab from the bottom pane of the selected virtual machine.

3. Select the virtual NIC and click on **Edit**; this will open an **Edit Network Interface** window.

4. Click on the **Profile** field and choose the VNIC profile from the drop-down menu and click on **OK**.

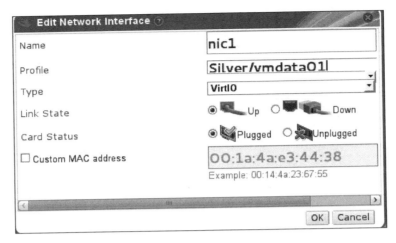

Hot plugging devices

Red Hat Enterprise Virtualization 3.3 supports hot plugs of additional virtual hard disks and virtual network interface card in running guests.

Hot plugging and removing virtual hard disks

To add an additional virtual hard disk to a running guest, use the following steps:

1. Log in to the **Administrator** console, navigate to the **Virtual Machines** resource tab, and select the appropriate virtual machine.

2. Navigate to the **Disks** tab from the bottom pane of the selected virtual machine.

3. Click on **Add**; this will open an **Add Virtual Disk** window.

4. Enter the size of the disk and make sure that the disk interface type is selected to **Virtio** not **IDE**. Full virtualization is a nice feature because it allows you to run any operating system virtualized. However, it's slow because the hypervisor has to emulate actual physical devices, such as RTL8139 network cards or IDE disks.

5. Virtio is a virtualization standard for networks and disk device drivers, where just the guest's device driver knows that it is running in a virtual environment and cooperates with the hypervisor. This enables guests to get high performance network and disk operations, and give most of the performance benefits of paravirtualization.

6. Fill in rest of the relevant fields as we did when we added a virtual disk to the virtual machine, and click on **OK**.

7. For a couple of seconds, the newly added disk will be in the **Locked** state before changing to the **Deactivated** state.

8. Select the newly added disk, and click on **Activate**.

9. Now you can log in to the guest operating system, and use the disk utility ships with the operating system to configure the new disk.

In the same way, we can also hot remove disk attached to the guest operating system. To remove the virtual hard disk online, perform these steps:

1. Deactivate the disk that is to be hot removed.

2. Finally, select **Remove** to remove it permanently.

Hot plugging in VNIC

Like hot plug and remove of virtual disk, RHEV supports hot plug and remove of VNIC to the virtual machine. To add an additional VNIC to a running guest, perform these steps:

1. Log in to the **Administrator** console, navigate to the **Virtual Machines** resource tab, and select the appropriate virtual machine.

2. Navigate to the **Network Interfaces** tab from the bottom pane of the selected virtual machine.

3. Click on **New**; this will open a **New Network Interface** window.

4. Fill in the relevant fields, and click on **OK** to add a new virtual network interface to the guest, and close the window.

Hot plugging virtual CPU

Starting with Red Hat Enterprise Virtualization 3.4 release supports hot plugging vCPUs into running guests to increase computing capacity. For more information, please refer to Red Hat Enterprise Virtualization 3.4 Administration Guide.

Summary

In this chapter, we discussed various advanced features of Red Hat Enterprise Virtualization, such as shareable or floating disks, direct LUN mapping, virtual hard disk resize, storage live migration of disk from one storage domain to another, implementing network quality of service using VNIC profiles, and hot plugging of virtual hard disks, virtual network adapters, and virtual CPUs.

In the next chapter, we will discuss implementing quota to limit the virtualization resource usage and integration of Red Hat Enterprise Virtualization with directory services so that directory users can be assigned different roles and permissions according to the tasks they have to perform in the virtualization infrastructure.

Quota and User Management

7

So far, we have created several running virtual machines and learned about various advanced features of Red Hat Enterprise Virtualization. In this chapter, we are going to learn the various user management techniques that have role-based access control for the multilevel administration of your virtual infrastructure. This is done by integrating RHEV-M with some common directory services and implementing Quota to limit the resource consumption of the virtual infrastructure.

In this chapter, we are going to learn the following topics:

- User management
- Integrating with directory services
- Introduction to Quota

An overview of user management

As an administrator, you have created several running virtual machines, and you can assign users to access the machines from the user portal. RHEV supports two types of user accounts: one is the admin account, which resides in the internal domain created during the RHEV-M installation, and other users are managed by integrating the manager with external directory services such as openLDAP, active directory services, and more for user authentication.

Except the internal admin account, the rest of the user accounts must be created in external directory servers, and these users are called directory users. Once the manager is attached to any of the supported directory servers, the users who reside in the directory servers can be added to the manager administration portal, thus making them RHEV-M users.

Using this multilevel administration feature of RHEV, we can customize permissions for each logical component, such as virtual machines, clusters, data centers, and more, to the RHEV-M users added to the administration portal from the directory servers.

There are two types of RHEV-M users: one is the end user who can access the virtual resources from the user or power user portal, and other is the administrative user who can manage and maintain the virtualization infrastructure using the admin portal. Users can be assigned different roles and permissions. For instance, in order to access a virtual machine from the user portal, a user must have either user role or power user role permissions for the virtual machine. These permissions are added from the manager administration portal. So, user roles and admin roles can be assigned to RHEV-M users in order to access individual resources such as virtual machines or hosts and to complete objects such as clusters or data centers.

Before diving into user roles and permission, we need to add users to RHEV-M, and to do this, you will need to attach a directory server to the manager using the domain management tool, called engine-manage-domains, installed as a part of the RHEV-M installation.

The directory servers supported for use with Red Hat Enterprise Virtualization 3.3 are the following:

- Active directory
- Identity Management
- Red Hat Directory Server 9
- OpenLDAP

There are certain DNS record prerequisites that must be configured in your DNS server in order to add the directory service domain to the RHEV-M configuration using engine-manage-domains. If you use IdM and follow the steps mentioned in the *Installing and configuring Red Hat IdM* section in *Chapter 10, Setting Up iSCSI, NFS, and IdM Directory Services for RHEV*, the required DNS records will be created automatically. Also, a user must be created in the directory server specifically for use as the RHEV administrative user. Do not use the administrative user for the directory server as the RHEV administrative user. Please refer to the *Directory Users* section from RHEV 3 Administration Guide for more details at `https://access. redhat.com/documentation/en-US/Red_Hat_Enterprise_Virtualization/3.3/ html/Administration_Guide/sect-Directory_Users.html`.

Adding the IdM domain to RHEV Manager

In this coming section, we are going to see how to attach a Red Hat Identity Management domain to RHEV-M and add directory users to RHEV-M users.

Refer to *Chapter 10, Setting Up iSCSI, NFS, and IdM Directory Services for RHEV*, to set up and configure the IdM domain on the RHEL server in order to use it with your RHEV-M running on your infrastructure.

> You can't install IdM on the same box as your running RHEV-M due to the `mod_ssl` package conflict, so you need to use a dedicated instance to run the IdM server, and it can be run as a virtual machine on your RHEV infrastructure too.

In the following example, we are going to add the IdM domain, which is configured and run on RHEL Version 6 Update 5, to RHEV-M. IdM is configured with the `example.com` domain name, and we are going to add this domain name by using the admin credentials of the IdM server using the engine-manage-domains utility installed on the manager system. For more options on using engine-manage-domains, please use the `--help` switch:

```
[root@rhevmanager ~]# engine-manage-domains    -action=add
-domain=example.com -provider=IPA -user=admin -interactive
Enter password:
The domain example.com has been added to the engine as an authentication
source but no users from that domain have been granted permissions within
the oVirt Manager.
Users from this domain can be granted permissions by editing the domain
using -action=edit and specifying -addPermissions or from the Web
administration interface logging in as admin@internal user.
oVirt Engine restart is required in order for the changes to take place
(service ovirt-engine restart).
Manage Domains completed successfully
[root@rhevmanager ~]#
```

Validating and listing added domains

To validate the configured domains, please run the following command:

```
[root@rhevmanager ~]# engine-manage-domains -action=validate
Domain example.com is valid.
The configured user for domain example.com is admin@EXAMPLE.COM
Manage Domains completed successfully
[root@rhevmanager ~]#
```

To list all the directory service domains defined in the RHEV-M configuration, please run the following command:

```
[root@rhevmanager ~]# engine-manage-domains -action=list
Domain: example.com
        User name: admin@EXAMPLE.COM
Manage Domains completed successfully
[root@rhevmanager ~]#
```

You need to restart the ovirt-engine service once for the changes to take effect in Manager Administrator Portal user login screen under domain field to show the list of the domains that Red Hat Enterprise Virtualization Manager is attached to. To restart ovirt engine service please run the below command:

```
[root@rhevmanager ~]# /sbin/service ovirt-engine restart
Stopping oVirt Engine:                                    [  OK  ]
Starting oVirt Engine:                                    [  OK  ]
[root@rhevmanager ~]#
```

Now, log out and reload the admin or user portal from your browser, and log in as the default internal admin account. We just added the directory services to the manager, and we need to add the directory users and assign roles and permission to the users.

Adding directory users

To add a directory user as a RHEV-M user, perform the following steps:

1. Log in to administrator portal as a default `admin@internal` user account.
2. Navigate to the **Users** resource tab, and click on **Add.** This will open a new **Add Users and Groups** window.
3. On the same window, select the `example.com` domain, in our case, from the drop-down menu of the **Search** field, and click on **GO**.

4. This will pull down all the users and groups residing in the `example.com` domain of the IdM server.

5. Select users by marking the users, and click on **OK** to add the selected user to manager, and then close the window.

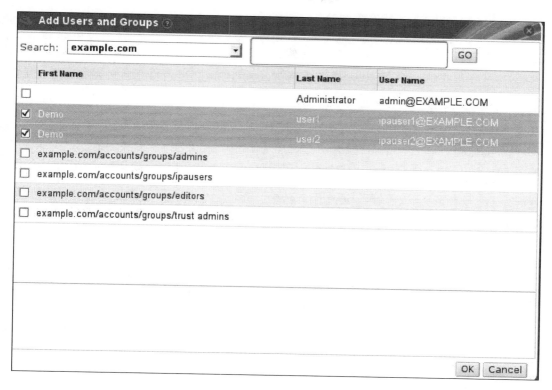

To view users and their information, perform the following steps:

1. Now, you can see the list of all the selected users visible under the **Users Resource** tab of the manager window.

2. Select any of the domain users, and navigate to all the subtabs, such as **General, Permissions, Quota, Directory Groups,** and **Event Notifier**, in the bottom pane. You can use **Event Notifier** to configure an e-mail alert as well.

3. Under the **Permissions** tab of the selected user, you can see that a few roles are assigned by default.

Authorizing users and assigning roles

RHEV applies user authorization controls based on three main aspects. The first aspect is the user who is performing the operation, type of action, and the object on which the action is being performed. RHEV uses the user-action-object model to assign permissions or roles.

To perform an action, the user must have the required permission for the object that is to be worked upon. The permission enables the user to perform some actions on either individual objects or container objects. Examples of individual objects are specific virtual machines, hosts, or a storage domain, and examples of container objects are data center or clusters in RHEV. Users who have permission to access container objects have permission to access all member objects of the container, such as storage, virtual machines, templates, and more.

RHEV provides a range of preconfigured roles, such as super user, power user, and more. You can't remove these roles; rather, you can clone the preconfigured roles and customize them based on your requirements from the manager admin portal for the administrator with system-wide access and specific virtual machine access to end users. In short, roles are a collection of permissions on RHEV.

The administrator role allows you to access the administration portal in order to manage physical and virtual resources. On the other hand, the user role will allow you to manage only a specific set of virtual machines and templates assigned to the user, and the power user role will allow you to create a virtual machine from the user portal. For a complete list of various user roles, please refer to the *Red Hat Enterprise Virtualization Manager User Properties and Roles* section from RHEV 3 Administration Guide at `https://access.redhat.com/documentation/en-US/Red_Hat_Enterprise_Virtualization/3.3/html/Administration_Guide/sect-Red_Hat_Enterprise_Virtualization_Manager_User_Properties_and_Roles.html`.

To assign power user role permissions to one of the users, named ipauser1, perform the following steps:

1. Log in to the administrator portal, and navigate to the **Users** tab.
2. Click on **Configure** from the top right-hand side of the header bar, and this will open a **Configure** window.
3. Move to the **System Permissions** tab, and click on **Add**. This will open the **Add System Permission to User** window.
4. Select the domain from the **Search** field's drop-down menu, in our case, `example.com`, and then click on **GO**.
5. This will filter out other domain users and return the list of users in the `example.com` domain. Select the user named **ipauser1**.

6. Select **PowerUserRole** from the **Role to Assign** drop-down menu, and then click on **OK** and close the tab.

7. Now, the **ipauser1** user permission is added with **PowerUserRole** under the **User** tab of the selected user.

8. Follow the same step and assign **UserRole** for the second directory user named **ipauser2**.

9. Now, navigate to `https://fqdn-of-manager/ovirt-engine/`, and click on the user portal and log in with the directory server user name, that is, **ipauser1**.

10. Cross-check the login to the same user portal as another directory user named **ipauser2**, and note the difference in the user portal options for the **ipauser2** user with the simple **UserRole** permission and the **ipauser1** user with the **PowerUserRole** permission.

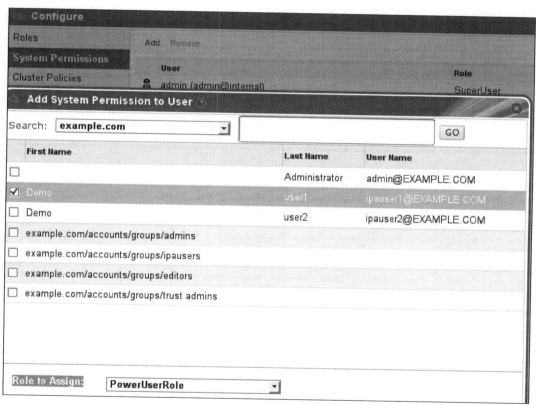

Creating a new role

RHEV allows you to define a custom role based on your requirements if the default roles do not suit your environment. Keep in mind that you can't delete the default roles; instead, you can create a new role or clone an existing role to match your requirements. To create a new role, perform the following steps:

1. Log in to the administrator portal, and click on **Configure** from the top right-hand side of the header bar. This will open the **Configure** window.

2. Under **Roles**, you can click on **New** to create a new role from scratch or select any of the existing roles and modify them as per your requirements before assigning the custom role to the users.

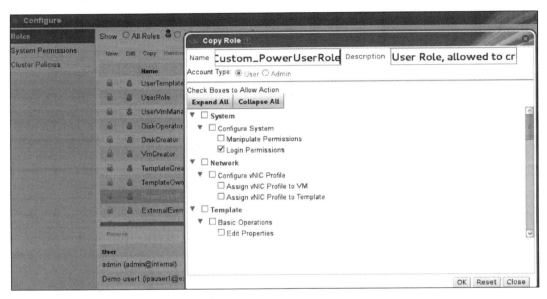

To understand various preconfigured user and administrator roles, please refer to the *User Roles Explained* section from RHEV 3 Administration Guide at `https://access.redhat.com/documentation/en-US/Red_Hat_Enterprise_ Virtualization/3.3/html-single/Administration_Guide/index.html#User_ Roles_Explained`.

Introduction to Quota

RHEV supports Quota; this is a data center object that will be used to limit the virtualization resource usage on top of the limitation set by the user permission. Quota allows you to limit memory, CPU, and storage disks. Quota can be assigned to individual users or groups so that whenever the user Quota limit reaches the defined limit, the users are forced to stop performing further actions.

RHEV supports two different kinds of Quota:

- **Run-time Quota**: This limits the consumption of resources such as CPU and memory
- **Storage Quota**: This limits the consumption of storage disks

RHEV Quota has three modes:

- **Audit**: Setting Quota on the data center in this mode will allow the admin to change both runtime and storage Quota based on the demand
- **Enforced**: Setting Quota to this mode will put it into effect and prevent users to further resources
- **Disabled**: This completely disables both runtime and storage Quota

RHEV Quota supports hard and soft limits and also allows the admin to define a threshold on the resources. This will be helpful in sending alerts to the user if the usage reaches the defined threshold in order to prevent failures when the user unexpectedly exceeds this threshold.

Whenever the user tries to start a virtual machine, virtual machine specifications are compared with the runtime and storage allowance set for Quota. If Quota reaches the maximum aggregated limit, then the manager will refuse to start the virtual machine.

When Quota is running in the enforced mode, virtual machines and disks that do not have assigned Quotas cannot be used. To power on a virtual machine, Quota must be assigned to that virtual machine.

Enabling Quota

In order to enable Quota and set the Quota mode in the data center, perform the following steps:

1. Log in to the administrator portal and navigate to the **Data Center** tab.
2. Select the data center on which you want to enable Quota.
3. Click on **Edit** in the top-left section of the navigation pane.

4. Change **Quota Mode** from **Disabled** to **Enforcing** or **Audit** and then click on **OK**.

5. A new warning window, **Change Datacenter Quota Enforcement Mode**, will pop up if you select the **Enforcing** mode. It's advised that you set the Quota mode to **Audit** initially to test and later change it to the **Enforcing** mode.

Creating the Quota policy

After enabling Quota and setting it to the audit or enforcing mode, you need to define a new Quota policy. To define a new Quota policy and apply it to the data center, perform the following steps:

1. Log in to the administrator portal, and navigate to the **Data Center** tab.

2. Select the data center and move it to the **Quota** tab that appears in the navigation pane.

3. Click on **Add**, and this will open the **New Quota** window where you can fill in the name for the new quota policy with a meaningful description.

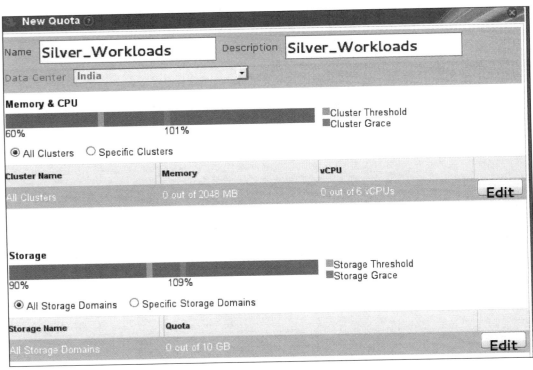

4. Under the **Memory & CPU** section of the window, use the green slider to set **Cluster Threshold** and the blue slider to set **Cluster Grace**. Optionally, you can select the specific cluster or choose the Quota applicable to all the clusters in the data center.

5. Under the **Memory & CPU** section of the same window, click on the **Edit** button in bottom-right corner and limit the memory and CPU from unlimited to a limit set by Quota.

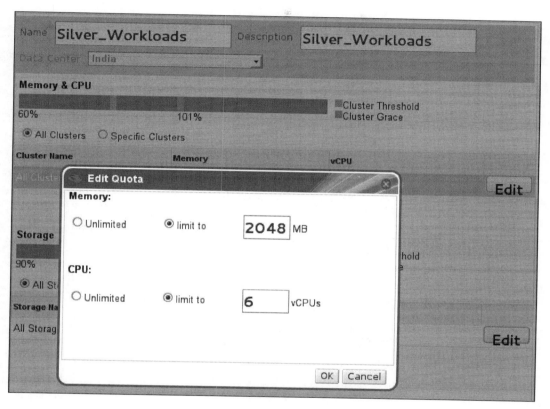

6. Under the **Storage** section of the same window, use the green slider to set **Storage Threshold** and the blue slider to set **Storage Grace**. Then, click on the **Edit** button in bottom-right corner, and limit the storage size from unlimited to a limit set by Quota.

   Here, the threshold is like the soft limit; exceeding this will generate a warning. Grace is like a hard limit and exceeding it will prevent further resource usage.

   Quota must be selected for all objects under the data center. For example, if you try to start a virtual machine, keeping Quota in the **Audit** mode, you will receive a warning stating that **Missing Quota for VM VMNAME, proceeding since in Permissive (Audit) mode** under the **Events** tab before the virtual machine is powered on. If Quota is set to the **Enforcing** mode, the virtual machine will fail to start unless Quota is selected for the virtual machine and its virtual disks.

Assigning Quota to virtual machine objects

To assign Quota to a virtual machine and its virtual disks, perform the following steps:

1. Log in to the administrator portal and navigate to the **Virtual Machine** tab.
2. Select the virtual machine and click on **Edit**. This will open the **Edit Virtual Machine** window.
3. Select the Quota to be consumed by the virtual machine from the drop-down menu and click on **OK**.
4. Next, we need to assign Quota to virtual machines' virtual disks.
5. Select the virtual machine, and move to the **Disks** tab of the selected virtual machine from the bottom pane.
6. Select the virtual disk, and click on **Edit**. In the **Virtual disk edit** window, select Quota from the drop-down menu and click on **OK**.

   Now, we have Quota applied to both virtual machines and their virtual hard disks. If you start the virtual machine now, then the Quota warning message will go away if the consumption does not exceed the threshold and Quota is set in the audit mode. If Quota is set in the enforcing mode, the manager will prevent you from starting the virtual machine if the Quota limit for the user or groups exceeds.

Assigning Quota to limit resources by users

To assign Quota to an individual user or group, perform the following steps:

1. Log in to the administrator portal, navigate to the **Quota** tab, and select Quota from the list.

2. Select **Consumers** from the bottom pane. This will open the **Assign user and Groups to Quota** window.

3. Choose the domain from the **Search** field's drop-down menu, and click on **GO**. Now, select the user to whom Quota will be assigned.

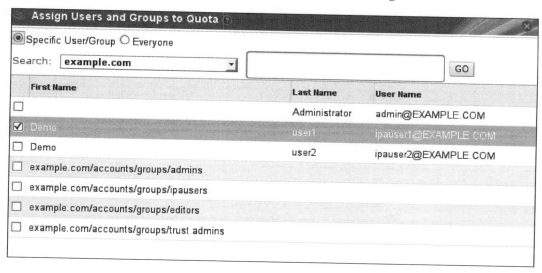

4. Now, log in with the user from the user portal, and try to create a virtual machine with the running resource and storage resource exceeding the defined threshold for Quota to be tested.

   If you set your Quota mode to audit, it will allow you to start your virtual machine even though the defined limit exceeds the threshold, and if the quota mode is set to enforcing, it will prevent you from starting a new virtual machine with the Quota exceed error.

Summary

In this chapter, we discussed user management in RHEV, integrating with directory services, adding the directory users as a RHEV-M user, and creating and assigning roles and permissions to access the individual or container objects from the user portal in detail. In the last section, we discussed how to implement Quota to limit the resource usage and apply Quota to users in order to limit the virtualization resource usage by users in RHEV.

The next chapter shows you how to set up the command-line tools other than web-based management to manage your virtualization infrastructure using the RHEV-M administration portal.

8

Managing a Virtualization Environment from the Command Line

So far, we have a full-fledged working virtualization infrastructure that is designed and executed on RHEV, with all the advanced features configured, ready, and managed from the administration and user portal of RHEV-M. In this chapter, we are going to learn how you can set up and use the command-line shell to manage your RHEV infrastructure, in addition to managing it from a graphical administrator console.

We are going to learn the following topics:

- Introduction to the **Command-Line Interface (CLI)**
- Installing and setting up the CLI
- Basic command-line examples

Introduction to the CLI

Red Hat Enterprise Virtualization supports the **CLI**, which allows users to connect to the RHEV-M system to manage their virtualization infrastructure apart from managing it from a standard administration graphical web interface. CLI also supports scripting, which will help administrators to perform periodic and repetitive tasks from their client machine.

Installing and setting up CLI

To install the command-line shell on the RHEL client, perform the following steps:

1. First, you need to register your manager machine to the Red Hat Network, and subscribe it to the relevant RHEV channel using the following commands:

```
# rhn_register
# rhn-channel --add –channel=rhel-x86_64-server-6-rhevm-3.3
```

It's strongly recommended that you use the Red Hat Subscription manager to register and subscribe to the relevant channel.
To use the Red Hat Subscription manager, please refer to the *Manager Installation* section under RHEV 3.3 Installation Guide at https://access.redhat.com/documentation/en-US/Red_Hat_Enterprise_Virtualization/3.3/html-single/Installation_Guide/index.html.

2. Install the CLI-related packages by running the following command:

```
#  yum install rhevm-cli -y
```

3. Once you have installed the CLI packages on the client machine, the next step is to obtain a certificate from the Red Hat Enterprise Virtualization Manager machine. Once this is done, store it in the certificate store of your client machine since the CLI installed on the client machine connects via **Hypertext Transfer Protocol Secure (HTTPS)** to access the **Application Programming Interface (API)** of RHEV-M.

If you are using a different client, please refer to the Red Hat Enterprise Virtualization Manager Release Notes available at https://access.redhat.com/documentation/en-US/Red_Hat_Enterprise_Virtualization/3.3/html/Manager_Release_Notes/index.html for specific channel names relevant to your system.

To obtain a certificate, perform the following steps:

1. You can use various methods to obtain the certificate, and in this chapter, we are going to use Wget, the common utility, that ships along with most of the Linux distribution.

> For detailed instructions on using other methods to obtain the certificate, please refer to the *TLS/SSL Certification* section under RHEV 3.3 Command Line Shell Guide at `https://access.redhat.com/documentation/en-US/Red_Hat_Enterprise_Virtualization/3.3/html/Command_Line_Shell_Guide/Attaining_an_SSL_certificate_from_RHEVM_for_a_REST_API_Client.html`.

2. To download and save the certificate using Wget, run the following command:

```
# wget -O rhevm.cer http://rhevmanager.example.com/ca.crt
```

3. Once you obtain the certificate on the client machine, you can start the CLI application by running the following command from an interactive shell:

```
[root@storage ~]# rhevm-shell
URL: https://rhevmanager.example.com/
Username: admin
Password:
```

4. Alternatively, in order to automatically connect to the shell, run the following command:

```
# rhevm-shell -c -l "https://rhevmanager.example.com/api"   -u
admin@internal -A /root/rhevm.cer
Password:"feed-your-admin-passowrd"

==========================================
 >>> connected to RHEVM manager 3.3.0.0 <<<
==========================================
+++++++++++++++++++++++++++++++++++++++++++
          Welcome to RHEVM shell
+++++++++++++++++++++++++++++++++++++++++++
[RHEVM shell (connected)]#
```

Basic command-line examples

CLI is an interactive shell, and the user can type in the required command and press *Tab* for autocomplete just like we do in Linux bash. To get the list of commands after you login to the CLI shell for the first time, press your *Tab* key twice. This will give you a list of all the commands, as shown in the following code:

```
[RHEVM shell (connected)]#

EOF          add          connect      disconnect    exit        help
info         ping         shell        status        update       action
clear        console      echo         file          history     list
remove       show         summary

[RHEVM shell (connected)]#
```

As an example, to list the virtual machines, you can type in `help` for the specific command, and this will open a help page on how to run the command with different options to get the output. Execute the following `help` command from the shell for VMS:

```
[RHEVM shell (connected)]# help list
[RHEVM shell (connected)]# help list vms
```

The output of the `help list vms` command is shown as follows:

```
This example lists all virtual machines:

    $ list vms

  - This example lists all virtual machines with all (not empty) properties,

    (by default only id/name/description properties displayed, using

    --show-all option, all not empty properties will be displayed,

    to see entire resource - use 'show' command)

    $ list vms --show-all

  - This example lists only virtual machines that have a name that starts

    with "myvm":

    $ list vms --query "name=myvm*"
```

To list all the virtual machines from the command shell, run the following command:

```
[RHEVM shell (connected)]# list vms
id           : ac102f18-3639-416f-a7ec-79d116ac173d
name         : baseclone
```

```
description: baseclone


id         : 9419a8f0-4a49-4254-a3e1-d728d21408a1
name       : quota_check
description: quota_check


id         : f5f6f570-5adc-410c-b210-48c315cf1747
name       : RHEL6Update5
description: RHEL Apache Web Server


id         : f84dcd4f-969c-455c-87bb-5e8eb67c3226
name       : Windows2008R2
description: Windows 2k8 IISServer
[RHEVM shell (connected)]#
```

To list a specific virtual machine with all its detailed properties from the command shell, run the following command:

```
RHEVM shell (connected)]# show vm baseclone
id                          : ac102f18-3639-416f-a7ec-79d116ac173d
name                        : baseclone
description                 : baseclone
cluster-id                  : a93ec6ff-aad4-460d-a2cd-6da733dc07a6
cpu-topology-cores          : 1
cpu-topology-sockets        : 1
cpu_shares                  : 0
creation_time               : 2014-04-21 06:36:45.959000-04:00
delete_protected            : True
display-allow_override      : False
display-monitors            : 1
display-single_qxl_pci      : True
display-smartcard_enabled   : False
display-type                : spice
high_availability-enabled   : False
high_availability-priority  : 1
memory                      : 1073741824
memory_policy-guaranteed    : 715128832
```

```
origin                       : ovirt
os-boot-dev                  : hd
os-type                      : rhel_6x64
placement_policy-affinity    : migratable
quota-id                     : bf2252cc-fbde-4ec6-ac00-9d20e5cf5a13
stateless                    : False
status-state                 : down
template-id                  : 00000000-0000-0000-0000-000000000000
type                         : server
usb-enabled                  : False
[RHEVM shell (connected)]#
```

Choose the command and press the *Tab* key twice to get the list of other available options passed on to the command:

```
[RHEVM shell (connected)]# list vms TAB TAB
```

Running Linux commands in a shell

Users can also run Linux shell commands or pipe the CLI command output to Linux shell commands from the RHEVM shell:

```
RHEVM shell (connected)]#  list vms --show-all > /root/vm_list.txt
```

Running commands with ! in front will execute the specified command on the local computer, so the following command lists the Linux shell command current directory of local computer listing by using the ! sign in front of the command in the shell:

```
[RHEVM shell (connected)]# !ls
anaconda-ks.cfg
install.log
install.log.syslog
rhevm.cer
vm_list.txt
[RHEVM shell (connected)]#
```

Listing resources from the command-line shell

To list the various Red Hat Enterprise Virtualization logical components such as data centers, clusters, logical networks, and virtual machine templates of your virtualization infrastructure, run the following commands respectively:

```
[RHEVM shell (connected)]#  list datacenters
[RHEVM shell (connected)]#  list clusters
[RHEVM shell (connected)]#  list networks
[RHEVM shell (connected)]#  list  templates
```

Creating and editing a virtual machine

In order to create and edit a virtual machine, use the following commands:

* To create a new virtual machine from CLI, use the existing virtual machine templates and run the following command:

  ```
  [RHEVM shell (connected)]# add vm --name vmfrmcli --descripton
  "virtual machine created from cli" --cluster-name Web-Cluster
  --template-name RHEL6Web
  ```

  This command will create a new virtual machine named vmfrmcli in a cluster named Web-Cluster from the existing virtual machine template RHEL6Web.

* To list a virtual machine that is currently powered on, run the following command. It's equivalent to searching the virtual machine, which is in the up status from the search bar of the admin portal:

  ```
  [RHEVM shell (connected)]# list vms --query "status=up"
  ```

* To list a virtual machine that is currently powered off, run the following command:

  ```
  [RHEVM shell (connected)]# list vms --query "status=down"
  ```

* To start a powered-down virtual machine, run the following command:

  ```
  [RHEVM shell (connected)]# action vm vmfrmcli start
  status-state: complete
  vm-id       : f7466164-8a80-4e11-b121-4e290876fc08
  [RHEVM shell (connected)]#
  ```

* To connect to a virtual machine console, run the following command:

  ```
  [RHEVM shell (connected)]# console  vmfrmcli
  ```

- To remove a virtual machine, disable the delete protection of the virtual machine first before attempting to remove the virtual machine. To disable the delete protection of a virtual machine, run the following command:

```
[RHEVM shell (connected)]# update vm vmfrmcli --delete_protected
False
```

- To force remove the virtual machine, run the following command:

```
[RHEVM shell (connected)]#  remove vm vmfrmcli --force
```

- Use the summary command to display a summary of the system status, as shown in the following command:

```
[RHEVM shell (connected)]# summary
```

- Use the EOF command to leave the CLI shell using a *Ctrl+D* sequence, as shown in the following code:

```
[RHEVM shell (connected)]# EOF
```

For more detailed information on using other resource types and the advanced CLI, please refer to Red Hat Enterprise Virtualization 3.3 Command Line Shell Guide at https://access.redhat.com/site/documentation/en-US/Red_Hat_Enterprise_Virtualization/3.3/html/Command_Line_Shell_Guide/index.html.

Summary

In this chapter, we discussed how to set up and install the CLI, and explored the basic command-line examples that are used to manage various virtual resources. The resources include managing the virtual machine and other resources such as data centers, clusters, host, and so on using the Red Hat Enterprise Virtualization CLI.

In the next chapter, we will talk about the various logfiles of RHEV-M, hypervisor hosts, and guest agents used to troubleshoot issues, and learn how to put your RHEV infrastructure in the maintenance mode for any planned outages.

9
Troubleshooting RHEV

In the previous chapters, we studied various command line examples to manage the Red Hat Enterprise Virtualization infrastructure. Now it's time to go through various troubleshooting techniques by referring to the various logs of the RHEV manager, hypervisor hosts, guest tool logs, and client-level logs to troubleshoot the SPICE connection of virtual machine consoles. We'll also look at the log collector utility and the steps to be performed to bring the Red Hat Enterprise Virtualization infrastructure to the maintenance state during the time of planned outage. In this chapter, we will cover the following topics:

- RHEV-M logs
- RHEV Hypervisor logs
- Guest agent and SPICE logs
- The log collector utility
- Maintaining an RHEV environment

RHEV Manager logs

All the logs related to the installation and initial setup, configuration, and database setup of RHEV-M, data warehouse, and report portal components are found under the /var/log/ovirt-engine/ directory of the RHEV-M system. You can use the following logs to troubleshoot the initial setup operation of various services such as RHEV-M, data warehouse, and reporting server:

- Complete information about the initial setup of the manager setup using the engine-setup command is shown in the following logfile:

  /var/log/ovirt-engine/setup/ovirt-engine-setup-yyyy_mm_dd_hh_ss.log

- Tracks of all the database-related setup information carried out as part of the oVirt engine setup installer are kept in the following logfile:

  `/var/log/ovirt-engine/engine-db-install-yyyy_mm_dd_hh_ss.log`

- Tracks of the initial `rhevm` data warehouse and report setup and the respective history database setup used to store the data for reporting are kept in the following logfile:

  `/var/log/ovirt-engine/rhevm-dwh-setup-yyyy_mm_dd_hh_ss.log`

  `/var/log/ovirt-engine/ovirt-engine-reports-setup-yyyy_mm_dd_hh_ss.log`

  `/var/log/ovirt-engine/ovirt-history-db-install-yyyy_mm_dd_hh_ss.log`

- All the information about ISO upload attempts using the `engine-iso-uploader` command installed as part of RHEV-M are stored in the following logfile:

  `/var/log/ovirt-engine/ovirt-iso-uploader/ovirt-iso-uploader-yyyy_mm_dd_hh_ss.log`

- All the information from the upload status of virtual machines in the **Open Virtualization Format (OVF)** image to export storage domains of the oVirt engine, also called as manager, are stored in the following logfile:

  `/var/log/ovirt-engine/ovirt-image-uploader/ovirt-image-uploader-yyyy_mm_dd_hh_ss.log`

- Messages related to the processing of the `engine-log-collector` command are contained in the following logfile. For more information on the log collector utility, please refer to *The log collector utility* section of this chapter:

  `/var/log/ovirt-engine/ovirt-log-collector/ovirt-log-collector-yyyy_mm_dd_hh_ss.log`

- All the domain-management-related information in the `engine-manage-domains` command line is tracked under the following logfile:

  `/var/log/ovirt-engine/engine-manage-domains.log`

- All the engine-configuration-related changes done in the `engine-config` command line are tracked under the following logfile:

  `/var/log/ovirt-engine/engine-config.log`

- Tracks of all RHEV-Manager-related logs, which include the hypervisor host reachability, UI access to the manager, and status of the manager database are kept by the following logfile:

  `/var/log/ovirt-engine/engine.log`

- All the oVirt engine data warehouses and Jasper report servers are logged under the following respective logfiles:

  `/var/log/ovirt-engine/ovirt-engine-dwhd.log`

  `/var/log/ovirt-engine/jasperserver.log`

- RHEV supports event notification by integrating the manager with your SMTP server so that in the case of specific events, respective alerts will be sent to the configured e-mail account via the configured SMTP server. All the event-notifier-related logs will be tracked under the following logfile:

  `/var/log/ovirt-engine/notifier/*.log`

- Tracks of all the installation and upgrade of packages associated with RHEV Manager are kept by the following logfile:

  `/var/lib/ovirt-engine/setup-history.txt`

- All the hypervisor hosts deployed using the manager will be tracked under the following logfile:

  `/var/log/ovirt-engine/host-deploy/ovirt-yyyy_mm_dd_hh_ss-host_ip_xyz.log`

RHEV Hypervisor hosts' logs

Most of the logs related to RHEV hypervisor hosts are logged in the hypervisor's `/var/log/vdsm` directory. For detailed information on the logs related to RHEV hypervisor hosts, please refer to the following list of logfiles:

- Complete information on the RHEV Hypervisor Host installation process can be found in the following logfile:

  `/var/log/ovirt.log`

- The complete list of information about the registration process of the RHEV Hypervisor host with RHEV Manager is stored in the following logfile:

  `/var/log/vdsm-reg/vdsm-reg.log`

- Logs under `vdsm.log` reflect the activity of the VDSM service, and this is the best place to troubleshoot the manager and hypervisor communication and more:

  `/var/log/vdsm/vdsm.log`

- All libvirt-service-related logs are tracked under `libvirtd.log`, where one can track the create, destroy, start, and stop statuses of virtual machines; they are stored in the following logfile:

  `/var/log/libvirt/libvirtd.log`

- Details of when the host has acquired, released, renewed, or failed to renew the storage pool manager lease are kept in the following logfile:

  `/var/log/vdsm/spm-lock.log`

Guest agent and SPICE logs

All guest-agent-related logs of the RHEL guest are found under `/var/log/ovirt-guest-agent/ovirt-guest-agent.log`.

If you are accessing the SPICE console of a virtual machine from the supported web browser of Windows 7 and RHEL clients, the respective logs will be found under the following:

- `Spice Client for Windows        Windows 7: %temp%\spicex.log`
- `Spice Client for RHEL    /var/log/messages`

The log collector utility

The log collector utility of RHEV allows users to gather the entire logs of your virtualization infrastructure or a custom collection of logs. This collection includes specific data centers, clusters, hosts, RHEV-M logs, and the RHEV database dump, which is useful to troubleshoot and analyze the root cause of any specific issue that you might come across on your virtualization stack.

To collect the complete logs of your entire virtualization infrastructure, run the following command:

```
[root@rhevmanager ~]# engine-log-collector
INFO: Gathering oVirt Engine information...
```

With the log collector utility, you can use the logs collected for your own analysis or to open a service request with Red Hat Global Support Service for any further assistance. Please refer to man page of `engine-log-collector` for more information on how to use various options.

Maintaining an RHEV environment

If you are planning to perform a scheduled maintenance of your IT infrastructure where Red Hat Enterprise Virtualization runs, you need to perform a certain task to bring your Red Hat Enterprise Virtualization infrastructure to the maintenance state.

The stop procedure

The following steps need to be performed in order to bring the Red Hat Enterprise Virtualization infrastructure to the maintenance state:

1. All the virtual machines should be powered off to avoid any data loss while performing maintenance.

2. Next, all the storage domains need to be put under the maintenance state. This can be done by navigating to the **Data Centers** tab and selecting the **data center** and **storage** subtabs in the bottom pane.

3. Select the storage domain and click on **Maintenance**. Please note that you must deactivate the **Master** storage domain in the end.

4. As the next step, you can mark the hypervisor host to the maintenance mode. To do so, navigate to the **Hosts** tab, select the host, and click on **Maintenance**. Once the host status is changed to **maintenance**, then you can safely shut down the host.

5. Finally, shut down RHEV Manager Server.

6. Optionally, you can also power down the storage.

The start procedure

Post your maintenance operation, you can start the Red Hat Enterprise Virtualization infrastructure by performing the following steps:

1. Power on the storage if it is powered off during the maintenance activity.

2. Once the storage is up and running, you can start all the hypervisor hosts.

3. Power on RHEV Manager Server once all the hypervisor hosts are up and running.

4. Activate the RHEV hypervisor host by navigating to the **Hosts** tab and clicking on **Activate**.

5. Once the hypervisor host is up and running, you need to again activate the storage domain back.

6. At least one data storage domain should be active before you activate the export or ISO domains. Upon activating the first data storage domain, one of the hypervisor hosts state will change from up to contending to become **Storage Pool Manager** (**SPM**).

7. Once the host gets an SPM status, the activated data domain will get the status of Master data domain.

8. Now you can start all the virtual machines and start your application.

Summary

In this chapter, we went through the various logfiles to troubleshoot any issues on the Red Hat Enterprise infrastructure. If you come across any issues related to networking and storage in manager, hypervisor, or virtual machines in your RHEV infrastructure, you can refer the specific logs explained in this chapter for your analysis and troubleshooting.

In the next chapter, we are going to discuss setting up various storage services and directory services on Red Hat Enterprise Linux to use with Red Hat Enterprise Virtualization.

10
Setting Up iSCSI, NFS, and IdM Directory Services for RHEV

In this chapter, we are going to discuss setting up various storage services and directory services to use with Red Hat Enterprise Virtualization. Generally, in any IT enterprise, a storage type of either **Network Attached Storage (NAS)**, iSCSI, or Fiber Channel is used to store critical application data and virtual machine images of the virtual infrastructure. From the point of view of directory services, they use either Active Directory Services in a Windows-dominated infrastructure and **Identity Management (IdM)** for Red Hat or OpenLDAP in a Linux-based infrastructure. Though you can use the local storage of the host to store virtual machine images for noncritical workloads with limited virtualization functionalities, such as the live migration of a virtual machine from one host to another, you can also turn your Red Hat Enterprise Linux server to **Network Attached Storage (NAS)** server, such as **Network File Server (NFS)** or iSCSI Server. Moreover, you can configure and set up the Red Hat IdM software to make the server act as a directory server for your Linux environment.

In this chapter, we are going to learn the following topics:

- How to set up iSCSI for the data domain
- How to set up NFS for the export domain
- How to install and configure IdM

In the forthcoming sections of the book, we are going to set up and configure NAS services on RHEL, such as iSCSI and NFS, for RHEV data and the export storage domain. We will also learn how to install and set up the IdM server for directory services to be attached with RHEV for user and group management.

Setting up iSCSI for the data domain

The following mentioned instructions are tested on RHEL 6 Update 5, and most of the steps, outlined as follows, work on both RHEL 5 Update 2 and higher and on RHEL 6. Please do the following:

1. Register the host to the Red Hat Network or create a local Yum repository, and install iSCSI-related packages.

2. Install `scsi-target-utils` packages with the following command:

   ```
   # yum install  scsi-target-utils -y
   ```

3. Identify the storage device to be used as a target, and use the Linux fdisk utility to partition the disk, which is 2 TB in size, as follows:

   ```
   # fdisk  /dev/sdb
   ```

4. To create a disk partition on a disk that is greater than 2 TB in size in Linux, use a utility called parted. To learn how to use parted, refer to `https://access.redhat.com/solutions/4281`. To learn more about using fdisk, refer to `https://access.redhat.com/documentation/en-US/Red_Hat_Enterprise_Linux/4/html/Introduction_To_System_Administration/s2-storage-addrem.html`.

5. Once you have created a new partition on the SDB device, use this new partition and create a logical volume, as follows:

   ```
   #  pvcreate  /dev/sdb1
   #  vgcreate  rhevsd /dev/sdb1
   # lvcreate  -L +49G -n datadisk1 rhevsd
   ```

   In the preceding example, `sdb1` was the partition you created using fdisk and then created a logical volume (lvm) of 49 GB.

6. Start the iSCSI target `tgtd` service and enable it to start when the system boots:

   ```
   #
   # /sbin/service tgtd start


   # chkconfig tgtd on
   For more information on tgtadm command line options please refer
   its man page by running below command as a root from the terminal
   of the storage server.

   # man tgtadm
   ```

7. Define a new iSCSI target name, as follows:

```
# tgtadm --lld iscsi --op new --mode target --tid=1   --targetname
rhev-data-disk-1:storage.example.com
```

8. Attach the 49 GB lvm block device that we created in the previous steps as your first logical unit to the target:

```
# tgtadm --lld iscsi --op new --mode logicalunit --tid 1 --lun 1
-b /dev/rhevsd/datadisk1
```

9. Define an access control for the newly created logical unit, and the following command will allow any iSCSI initiators to access it:

```
# tgtadm --lld iscsi --op bind --mode target --tid 1 -I ALL
```

> It's highly recommended to restrict target access to the required client IP address to prevent unauthorized usage of the target. In your case, you need to restrict access to all the hypervisor host storage logical network subnets or IPs.

10. To view the current configuration, run the following command:

```
# tgtadm --lld iscsi --op show --mode target
```

11. Finally, make sure that the TCP port 3260 is accessible from all the hypervisor host storage logical network segment IPs.

12. From RHEL 5.3 and higher, you can use the `tgt-admin` command line to dump the target configuration and redirect to the configuration file to make the target configuration persist across the reboot. Take a look at the following commands:

```
[root@storage ~]# tgt-admin   --dump

default-driver iscsi

<target rhev-data-disk-1:storage.example.com>

        backing-store /dev/rhevsd/datadisk1

</target>

[root@storage ~]# tgt-admin --dump > /etc/tgt/targets.conf
```

It's done! You have now configured the iSCSI target and can use this target for your data domain in the RHEV infrastructure from the RHEV-M administration portal **Storage** tab.

 Don't look for the iSCSI target using the iSCSI command-line utility from the hypervisor host's command line. All the addition or removal in the storage domain is to be performed only from the RHEV-M graphical interface.

Setting up NFS for the export domain

Once you have your RHEV up and running with the first data domain up and active, you can attach an NFS export as an export domain to back up your virtual machines and templates. The following section shows you how to set up a basic NFS in RHEL for your export domain in RHEV. Perform the following steps:

1. Register the host to the Red Hat Network or create a local Yum repository and install the NFS-related packages, as follows:

   ```
   # yum install nfs-utils -y
   ```

2. Create directories from the existing mount point to use them as export disks:

   ```
   # mkdir /export/rhev_import_export_disk
   ```

3. Export the disk in the NFS exports file and run the following command to export the mount point named /export/rhev_import_export_disk to all the disks with the few customized export options. Refer to man exports for detailed information on the export options used, as follows:

   ```
   # echo ""/export/rhev_import_export_disk *(rw,sync,no_subtree_
   check,all_squash,anonuid=36,anongid=36)"" >> /etc/exports
   ```

4. Empty the directory by removing all the files in the directory. Make sure to create a backup of the directory if there is any important data in it before running the following command:

   ```
   # rm -rf /export/rhev_import_export_disk/*
   ```

5. Set the user and group permission to 36:36, which is mandatory, for all NFS export disks to be attached in RHEV. Take a look at the following command:

   ```
   # chown 36:36 /export/rhev_import_export_disk/
   ```

6. Start the required NFS services and enable all NFS related services to start when the system boots, as follows:

```
# /etc/init.d/rpcbind  start ; /etc/init.d/nfs start ; /etc/
init.d/nfslock start

# /sbin/service rpcbind  start ; /sbin/service nfs start ; /sbin/
service nfslock start


# chkconfig  rpcbind on ; chkconfig  nfs on ; chkconfig nfslock on
```

7. Type the following command to list the shared directories from the NFS server. Run this command from all the hypervisor hosts' command lines to make sure the exported NFS mount point is accessible by the host before attaching it as an export domain:

```
[root@storage ~]#  showmount  -e storage.example.com
Export list for storage.example.com:
/export/rhev_import_export_disk *
[root@storage ~]#
```

The NFS export disk is now configured and ready to be attached as an export disk in the RHEV infrastructure from the RHEV-M administration portal **Storage** tab.

Installing and configuring Red Hat IdM

In this section, we are going to see how to install Red Hat Identity Management Server on Red Hat Enterprise Linux Version 6 Update 5.

Once IdM is installed, we will set up and configure the domain and DNS services and create directory users from the command line.

Finally, we will attach the newly configured IdM domain to the RHEV infrastructure and add directory users as RHEV-M users for the multilevel administration of your Red Hat Enterprise Virtualization infrastructure.

Refer to the identity management guide for your corresponding operating system version's minimal prerequisites from the Red Hat documentation portal. The mentioned instructions are tested on RHEL Version 6 Update 5. Please perform the following:

1. Install RHEL Version 6 Update 5 on a physical or virtual machine.

2. Select minimal installation during the package selection and register to the Red Hat network or create a local Yum repository.

3. Set up static networking with a Fully Qualified Domain Name and sync the system time with any of your NTP servers.

4. Disable the firewall and, optionally, disable SELinux if required.

5. Install the required IdM server packages by running the following command:

   ```
   # yum install ipa-server bind bind-dyndb-ldap
   ```

6. Now, to set up and configure your domain with the DNS service enabled, run the following command. Check man `ipa-server-install` for the various command-line options that can be used when running the following `ipa-server-install` command:

> We disabled the NTP service provided by IdM since we configured IdM on virtual machines. It's not advisable to set up the NTP server on virtual machines due to known time drift issues. The following command is interactive and will ask you a series of questions, and most of them are self-explanatory; you can either leave it as the default or customize it to make it relevant to your environment.

```
[root@ipa etc]# ipa-server-install  --setup-dns --no-ntp
The log file for this installation can be found in /var/log/
ipaserver-install.log
================================================================
============
This program will set up the IPA Server.
This includes:
    * Configure a stand-alone CA (dogtag) for certificate management
    * Create and configure an instance of Directory Server
    * Create and configure a Kerberos Key Distribution Center (KDC)
    * Configure Apache (httpd)
    * Configure DNS (bind)


Excluded by options:
    * Configure the Network Time Daemon (ntpd)


To accept the default shown in brackets, press the Enter key.
Existing BIND configuration detected, overwrite? [no]: yes
Enter the fully qualified domain name of the computer
on which you're setting up server software. Using the form
<hostname>.<domainname>
Example: master.example.com.
```

Server host name [ipa.example.com]:

Warning: skipping DNS resolution of host ipa.example.com

The domain name has been determined based on the host name.

Please confirm the domain name [example.com]:

The kerberos protocol requires a Realm name to be defined.

This is typically the domain name converted to uppercase.

Please provide a realm name [EXAMPLE.COM]:

Certain directory server operations require an administrative user.

This user is referred to as the Directory Manager and has full access

to the Directory for system management tasks and will be added to the

instance of directory server created for IPA.

The password must be at least 8 characters long.

Directory Manager password:

Password (confirm):

The IPA server requires an administrative user, named 'admin'.

This user is a regular system account used for IPA server administration.

IPA admin password:

Password (confirm):

Do you want to configure DNS forwarders? [yes]:

Enter the IP address of DNS forwarder to use, or press Enter to finish.

Enter IP address for a DNS forwarder:

No DNS forwarders configured

Do you want to configure the reverse zone? [yes]:

Please specify the reverse zone name [100.168.192.in-addr.arpa.]:

Using reverse zone 100.168.192.in-addr.arpa.

The IPA Master Server will be configured with:

Hostname: ipa.example.com

IP address: 192.168.100.84

Domain name: example.com

Realm name: EXAMPLE.COM

BIND DNS server will be configured to serve IPA domain with:

Forwarders: No forwarders

```
Reverse zone:   100.168.192.in-addr.arpa.

Continue to configure the system with these values? [no]: yes

The following operations may take some minutes to complete.

Please wait until the prompt is returned.
```

7. Once you've configured the domain and DNS service using IdM, check the IdM service status by running the following command:

```
[root@ipa ~]# ipactl  status

Directory Service: RUNNING

KDC Service: RUNNING

KPASSWD Service: RUNNING

DNS Service: RUNNING

MEMCACHE Service: RUNNING

HTTP Service: RUNNING

CA Service: RUNNING

[root@ipa ~]#
```

Now, we are good to create a few directory server users in IdM as well as domain name service records, if required, for the domain by accessing the IdM Web UI from supported browsers. To access the web UI, perform the following steps:

1. To enable web UI access from the browser, edit the /etc/httpd/conf.d/ ipa.conf file using the Vim editor and make the following changes:

```
# Protect /ipa and everything below it in webspace with Apache
Kerberos auth

<Location ""/ipa"">

  AuthType Kerberos

  AuthName ""Kerberos Login""

  KrbMethodNegotiate on

  KrbMethodK5Passwd on  ###<<<--- Change this line from ""off"" to
""on""

  KrbServiceName HTTP

  KrbAuthRealms EXAMPLE.COM

  Krb5KeyTab /etc/httpd/conf/ipa.keytab

  KrbSaveCredentials on

  KrbConstrainedDelegation on

  Require valid-user

  ErrorDocument 401 /ipa/errors/unauthorized.html

</Location>
```

2. To ensure that the preceding changes are reflected, restart HTTPD or the ipactl service with the following command:

```
# ipactl  restart
```

3. To open the web UI, go to `https://ipa.example.com/ipa/ui`.

4. Log in with the directory server login credentials configured when IdM was being set up to create users and the forward and reverse lookup zones of your DNS.

For the sake of simplicity, the examples in the following section demonstrate how we can create users from the command-line interface of the IdM server.

Adding users from CLI

Proceed with the following steps:

1. Log in as the root of the IdM server, and further log in as the admin user of the directory server to create additional users. Take a look at the following examples:

```
[root@ipa ~]# kinit admin@EXAMPLE.COM

Password for admin@EXAMPLE.COM:

[root@ipa ~]#  ipa user-add ipauser1 --first=Demo --last=user1
--password

Password:

Enter Password again to verify:

--------------------

Added user ""ipauser1""

--------------------

   User login: ipauser1

   First name: Demo

   Last name: user1

   Full name: Demo user1

   Display name: Demo user1

   Initials: Du

   Home directory: /home/ipauser1

   GECOS field: Demo user1

   Login shell: /bin/sh

   Kerberos principal: ipauser1@EXAMPLE.COM

   Email address: ipauser1@example.com
```

```
UID: 945200001
GID: 945200001
Password: True
Kerberos keys available: True
[root@ipa ~]#
```

2. Log in as the newly created user, and you will be asked to reset the password once. You are required to change the password of the IdM user once after the user is created in IdM to be able to log in to the RHEV admin or user portal. Take a look at the following example:

```
[root@ipa ~]# kinit ipauser1@EXAMPLE.COM
Password for ipauser1@EXAMPLE.COM:
Password expired.  You must change it now.
Enter new password:
Enter it again:
[root@ipa ~]#
```

For more detailed information on modifying user accounts and adding DNS records from the web UI or CLI, refer to the RHEL 6 Identity Management Guide at https://access.redhat.com/documentation/en-US/Red_Hat_Enterprise_Linux/6/html/Identity_Management_Guide/index.html.

Summary

In this chapter, we learned how to set up iSCSI and NFS storage on Red Hat Enterprise Linux to use it with Red Hat Enterprise Virtualization for various storage domains such as data, ISO, and export. Finally, we learned how to install and configure the Red Hat Identity Management server to act as a directory server to be attached to RHEV for multilevel user administration.

Index

Thank you for buying
Getting Started with Red Hat Enterprise Virtualization

About Packt Publishing

Packt, pronounced 'packed', published its first book "*Mastering phpMyAdmin for Effective MySQL Management*" in April 2004 and subsequently continued to specialize in publishing highly focused books on specific technologies and solutions.

Our books and publications share the experiences of your fellow IT professionals in adapting and customizing today's systems, applications, and frameworks. Our solution based books give you the knowledge and power to customize the software and technologies you're using to get the job done. Packt books are more specific and less general than the IT books you have seen in the past. Our unique business model allows us to bring you more focused information, giving you more of what you need to know, and less of what you don't.

Packt is a modern, yet unique publishing company, which focuses on producing quality, cutting-edge books for communities of developers, administrators, and newbies alike. For more information, please visit our website: www.packtpub.com.

About Packt Open Source

In 2010, Packt launched two new brands, Packt Open Source and Packt Enterprise, in order to continue its focus on specialization. This book is part of the Packt Open Source brand, home to books published on software built around Open Source licenses, and offering information to anybody from advanced developers to budding web designers. The Open Source brand also runs Packt's Open Source Royalty Scheme, by which Packt gives a royalty to each Open Source project about whose software a book is sold.

Writing for Packt

We welcome all inquiries from people who are interested in authoring. Book proposals should be sent to author@packtpub.com. If your book idea is still at an early stage and you would like to discuss it first before writing a formal book proposal, contact us; one of our commissioning editors will get in touch with you.

We're not just looking for published authors; if you have strong technical skills but no writing experience, our experienced editors can help you develop a writing career, or simply get some additional reward for your expertise.

Kali Linux Network Scanning Cookbook

ISBN: 978-1-78398-214-1   Paperback: 452 pages

Over 90 hands-on recipes explaining how to leverage custom scripts and integrated tools in Kali Linux to effectively master network scanning

1. Learn the fundamentals behind commonly used scanning techniques.

2. Deploy powerful scanning tools that are integrated into the Kali Linux testing platform.

3. A step-by-step guide, full of recipes that will help you use integrated scanning tools in Kali Linux, and develop custom scripts for making new and unique tools of your own.

Windows Server 2012 Hyper-V: Deploying Hyper-V Enterprise Server Virtualization Platform

ISBN: 978-1-84968-834-5   Paperback: 410 pages

Build Hyper-V infrastructure with secured multitenancy, flexible infrastructure, scalability, and high availability

1. A complete step-by-step Hyper-V deployment guide, covering all Hyper-V features for configuration and management best practices.

2. Understand multitenancy, flexible architecture, scalability, and high availability features of new Windows Server 2012 Hyper-V.

Please check **www.PacktPub.com** for information on our titles

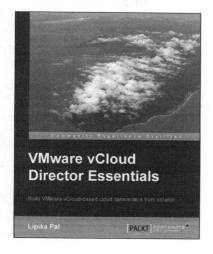

VMware vCloud Director Essentials

ISBN: 978-1-78398-652-1   Paperback: 198 pages

Build VMware vCloud-based cloud datacenters from scratch

1. Learn about DHCP, NAT, and VPN services to successfully implement a private cloud.

2. Configure different networks such as Direct connect, Routed, or Isolated.

3. Configure and manage vCloud Director's access control.

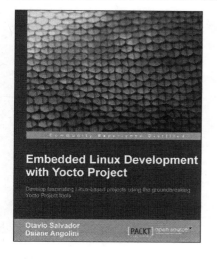

Embedded Linux Development with Yocto Project

ISBN: 978-1-78328-233-3   Paperback: 142 pages

Develop fascinating Linux-based projects using the groundbreaking Yocto Project tools

1. Optimize Yocto Project's capabilities to develop captivating embedded Linux projects.

2. Facilitates efficient system development by helping you avoid known pitfalls.

3. Demonstrates concepts in a practical and easy-to-understand way.

Please check **www.PacktPub.com** for information on our titles

Made in the USA
Lexington, KY
11 October 2017